The GPS for Writing

Grammar, Punctuation, and Structure

Jane Tainow Feder

Kendall Hunt
publishing company

Cover images © 2012, Shutterstock, Inc.
Cover design by Andy Feder

Kendall Hunt
publishing company

www.kendallhunt.com
Send all inquiries to:
4050 Westmark Drive
Dubuque, IA 52004-1840

Dedication

I dedicate this book to my children, Andy and Sam, with forever love and to my parents, Nettie Yeskel Tainow and Philip Tainow, with enduring love and gratitude for opening doors for me not available to them.

Table of Contents

4. Sentence Parts (CVS)   43

5. Sentence Types   73

6. Sentence Patterns   77

7. Punctuation [P]   97

8. Diagramming Sentences [GPS]   123

Acknowledgments

In preparing the 2nd edition of *The GPS for Writing: Grammar, Punctuation, and Structure*, I reviewed every page of the 1st edition including "Acknowledgements." I have decided to keep this page as it was first written; without the encouragement of family, friends, colleagues, and students, I would still be thinking that writing *The GPS* would be lovely—but impossible. Of inestimable value have been my forty-plus years of working with extraordinary people—my students and colleagues—who have enriched my life. I'm grateful to my children, Andy and Sam, and sister, Temma, for their encouragement to take on this project. Andy's keen sense of design and stunning photos add a rich dimension to the text. The gentle nudging, encouragement, and sound counsel from Mária Cipriani have been invaluable gifts during this journey. Lowell Scheiner's sharing his well-honed understanding of grammar and syntax gives the imprimatur to my work. I extend my gratitude to colleagues: Nina Bannett, Caroline Chamberlin Hellman, Charles Hirsch, Laura Kodet, Rob Ostrom, and Joan Poelvoorde. I offer heartfelt thanks to Marilyn and Harrison M. Davis III, Lori Kemper, and Dimitri and Carroll Vinson who bring sunshine and chocolates into my day. Finally, I offer my gratitude and affection to my lifelong friends Janet Cohen, for hours of fastidious and thoughtful editing, and to Fran Cohen Musler and Terri Berlin Acrish for helping me recognize that I have something valuable to share.

I am especially pleased to acknowledge contributions to this text from my students:

José De la Rosa	Jovian Rutherford
Ayodele Finch	Elias Salaam
Elsa Hadad	Godfrey Sakyi
Daniel Huerta	Fred Worell
Chein-chang Peter Li	Amer Yahia
Mario Leopold	and from Dimitri Vinson

I hope you enjoy *The GPS for Writing* as much as I enjoyed writing it.

The Guide for Writers and Writing Instructors

Dear Writer,

I'd like to demystify the rules for **g**rammar, **p**unctuation, and structure (*GPS*). There are no secrets or hidden tricks. These rules are logical. I know you can understand them. Just take this book one step at a time. If something is unclear, reread the explanation. Once you think the material is clear, try the short exercises at the end of each chapter. Then, check your answers right away; don't walk away thinking something is incorrect when you are right! Also, you want to correct any misconceptions you hold.

Whom does *The GPS for Writing* address?

The Audience

I have worked with writers from junior high school through graduate school. All writers want to know how to improve their writing. Some fortunate writers have always spoken well. Because they write the way they speak, their writing is effective. However, they don't know why it's good or how to make it even better. Some hopeful writers are eager to communicate their stories, but they don't know how to manipulate words and sentences to engage their readers. Few know the mechanics of writing. So, for whom is this book written? It's for all writers who want to understand the rules of grammar, punctuation, and structure to enhance their ability to communicate in writing.

How is *The GPS for Writing* organized?

The Chapters

The GPS is organized into chapters. In addition to "Overview" and "Proofreading," there are seven chapters with explanations of grammar, punctuation, and structure rules.

Each chapter includes exercises to check your understanding and web sites to give further explanation and practice. Each of the chapters is comprehensive in covering the mechanics of good writing. Look at the "Table of Contents," and you'll be impressed! See how much is covered in so few pages. It's all here at your fingertips; it's clear and user-friendly, including lots of examples, playful ways to remember rules, and photographs of sites in New York City, the terrain of southern California, my son rock climbing and deep-sea diving, and my daughter moving into a hand stand!

How might you begin using *The GPS?*

Whether going to work, to school, to a film, or to a club, you have to plan how you will get there. Mastering the mechanics of writing also requires a plan. As you read through the "Overview," you will see that I take you from **words** to **words functioning in sentences** to **types** and **patterns of sentences** to the composing process, and, finally, to proofreading symbols. Although there are chapters titled "Punctuation" and "Word Choices," the correct use of punctuation marks and appropriate choice of words are reviewed in other chapters as well.

Diagnostic Materials

If you plan to go through the entire *The GPS for Writing,* start with the pre-test. The "Table of Contents" will guide you to the page. When you check your answers, your strengths will become clear. You can, of course, choose to do only those chapters where your skills showed as weak. Once you feel you have finished your study, try the post-test. Compare the results of the post-test to the pre-test. My hunch is that you will have mastered the skills that were revealed as deficient on the pre-test.

These grammar, punctuation, and structure concepts may be challenging to grasp; however, I know that you can learn them. Once you, too, are convinced that you can learn these concepts, proceed with deliberation, focus, and time for review. Additionally, I know that your writing will improve through your mastery of these concepts as long as you proofread. You and I will make mistakes in our writing; however, proofreading will save us from showing those mistakes to others.

Just as I emphasize proofreading throughout the writing process, I urge you to take time to reflect while traveling through this guide. Set aside about 60-90 minutes for each session; clearly, some may need more time, others less. You needn't memorize all that's here; it's enough to know that you can always refer to this guide when questions arise.

Now, with an understanding of my philosophy as expressed in *The GPS for Writing* and your commitment to learning these concepts and knowing where to find the answers to your questions, let's move on.

Session 1—Chapter 14 "Pre-test Exercises and Answers"

Note—Chapter 1 gives an "Overview" of my way of teaching grammar. Chapter 2, "Proofreading," details the importance of continuously reading what you write. I urge you to read these chapters to get yourself going!
1. Let's find out what you know about grammar, punctuation, and structure. The "Pre-test Exercises" will help you to diagnose your writing strengths.
   The answers for all exercises are at the end of this guide.
2. The "Pre-test Exercises" will give you a baseline against which to measure your progress as you move through *The GPS for Writing*. The "Post-test Exercises" will confirm that you have mastered the concepts you studied.

Session 2—Chapter 3 "Words"

1. Learn that grammar is accessible.
2. Experiencing in just a few minutes that you can identify the eight parts of speech will reassure you that you can master the concepts in *The GPS for Writing*.
3. All you have to do is remember A V CAPPIN. Reciting each of these letters will help you to remember which words they represent. For example, A = Adjective; V = Verb. Read Chapter 3 to learn what the rest of the mnemonic stands for.
4. Remembering the names and correct spelling of these parts of speech at this time is good enough. We'll save the definitions for next session.

Session 3—Chapter 3 "Words"

1. Review the mnemonic A V CAPPIN and the words these letters represent to confirm that you have already started learning grammar.
2. Now, let's begin to define, in general terms, the eight parts of speech.
3. Once the definition is clear, give examples of each part of speech.
4. Some words function as several different parts of speech depending on their use in a sentence. This will become clear in Sessions 6-7.

Session 4-5—Chapter 3 "Words"

1. The most important part of speech is verbs (predicates). This is the only part of speech that can stand alone as a sentence. An example is "Run!" This is discussed in *The GPS for Writing*.
2. Verbs tell time or tense. Look at the twelve tenses; look at the time line. Once you make sense of the time line, work on understanding the tenses.
3. Taking verbs through the tenses is particularly challenging when working with irregular verbs. Regular verbs are more predictable.
4. Conjugating verbs, especially in the present tense, will help you to remember to put that "S" on the third person singular form. If this doesn't make sense to you now, don't worry; it will make sense when you read the chapter.
5. All verbs tell tense. Some verbs tell action, too. Some verbs do not tell action; they only express tense, for example "I **am** tall." You will learn about transitive, intransitive, and intransitive linking verbs (also Chapter 4).

Session 6-7—Chapter 4 "Sentence Parts"

1. Here's where you will move words into sentences and learn that a sentence is defined as a group of words with a complete thought, verb, subject. I'll ask you to remember CVS, a sure way of recalling the parts of a sentence.
2. Next, you will identify which parts of speech can act as subjects (nouns, pronouns).
3. You need to know the definitions of phrases and clauses and how they differ from a sentence—if they do. Actually, some clauses are sentences. You'll learn all about this in Chapter 4.
4. You will see that adjectives and adverbs bring vitality into sentences.
5. You will review degrees of adjectives and adverbs. Degrees of adjectives and adverbs, which create comparisons and contrasts, are reviewed.
6. As you learn about transitive verbs, you will learn about direct and indirect objects. At that point, you will find out about other

grammatical structures that include objects.

7. Along with transitive verbs will be the study of intransitive and intransitive linking verbs. Subject complements follow linking verbs. In Chapter 8, you will learn to diagram all of these parts of the sentence.

Session 7-8—Chapters 4-5 "Sentence Patterns" and "Sentence Types"

1. You will learn to identify common sentence errors and ways to correct them.
2. You will learn that subjects and verbs as well as pronouns and their antecedents must agree.
3. You will be given an explanation of pronoun references and pronoun cases.
4. Every sentence is one of four types.
5. You will practice writing one idea in each of the different types of sentences.

Session 9-10—Chapter 6 and 13 "Sentence Patterns" and "Glossary"

1. In session 7-8, Chapter 4, you looked at common sentence errors. In this chapter, you will learn about sentence patterns: simple, compound, complex, and compound/complex.
2. You will learn about conjunctions; they join parts of sentences and help to create sentence variety. Varied sentence structure enhances your writing and will help you to effectively engage your reader.
3. Once you understand the construction of sentence patterns, you will learn about common sentence structure errors: fragments, comma splices, and run-on sentences (also known as fused sentences).
4. Then, you will want to know how to correct these errors, and I'll give you several solutions for each error.
5. Note—Chapter 13 offers a "Glossary," which includes definitions of some of the most important words in the study of grammar.

Session 11—Chapter 7 "Punctuation"

1. You may want your writing to flow. Sometimes you may want to provoke the reader. Knowing when and where to use punctuation marks will help you to create a variety of effects through your writing.
2. You'll learn the rules that govern the use of punctuation marks, and you'll learn to use such marks sparingly.
3. Finally, you will become the master of the apostrophe! You'll know how to use it to show possession and to show omission of letters.

Session 12-13—Chapters 8-9 "Diagramming Sentences" and "Word Choices"

1. If you are a visual learner, if you enjoy reading graphs, if you like puzzles, you will really have fun diagramming sentences.
2. Through diagramming sentences, you will see how words interact with one another.
3. Language lives! Language is not static. New words are frequently introduced into dictionaries, and new ways of using familiar words are created. Have you "friended" anyone recently?" Using "friend" as a verb as well as a noun is new with Facebook.
4. You will learn about gender-neutral language.
5. You will find tips to help you improve your spelling.
6. Increasing your vocabulary will improve your writing. It will allow you to be more precise with your language choices.
7. As new words are created and existing words take on new meanings, their placement in the diagram changes to reflect their new functions.

Session 13—Chapter 9 "Word Choices"

Session 14 Chapters 10-12 "Facing the Blank Page," Structuring the Essay," and "Proofreading Marks"

1. Discussion of the fear of writing.
2. Reality checks to assess writing competence.
3. Proofreading for CUE=coherence, unity, and emphasis.
4. Proofreading marks are included to assure the students easy and understandable access to instructor's marking system

Chapters 15, 16, and 17 "Post-test Exercises and Answers," Answers to Chapter Exercises," and Web Sites to complement *The GPS for Writing"*

Note—Chapter 16, as you know by now, gives the answers, in alphabetical order, to all of the exercises within the chapters. Chapter 17 details the helpful web sites for additional review and practice.

1. Take the "Post-test Exercises" and compare the results of both the post-test and pre-test to confirm your mastery of the concepts covered in *The GPS*.
2. If you are not satisfied with the results, no problem; go back to the chapter, and try it again, or go to the suggested web sites, and have fun with songs and games, and I know you'll get it!

3. Helpful Web Sites have been added to complement the text and to encourage further exploration of the Web for additional exercises

What do I want to accomplish?

It is my hope that *The GPS for Writing* will help you to develop a positive relationship with words. I would like you to have confidence in your writing ability based on your demonstrating that you can write correct sentences in a variety of types and patterns. When you proofread your writing, I would like you to feel assured that you are clearly and effectively communicating your ideas. I want this for you because I know you want this, too!

A Note for Instructors

When teaching with *The GPS for Writing*, I recommend frequent and short 5-10 minute quizzes with 5-10 items marked by the instructor and, when students are ready, marked by students. Marking each other's papers will give the students additional exposure to the material. Assign code names to students to protect the innocent! Keeping all quizzes in an exam booklet will allow the learner to keep track of success.

Rely on the chapters in *The GPS for Writing* for definitions, examples, quizzes, and answers. You may want to create your own quick quizzes depending on how often you choose to check students' understanding of the material. Addresses for web sites are given in each chapter and in the back of the guide. Use these sites and refer your students to these sites for further explanation and practice. Many sites are very entertaining; some include songs that may help your students remember challenging rules.

The "Overview" will explain and show in a chart how I teach the mechanics of writing. The chapters are organized based on the sequence of steps that I believe will help your students master these basic skills. Each session, as described above, will need from 60-90 minutes.

If you would like to discuss any of the material in *The GPS for Writing*, contact me through email: jfeder@citytech.cuny.edu

Thank you for choosing *The GPS for Writing*,
Jane

Where do you want to go?

Chapter 1

An Overview

The GPS for Writing

GRAMMAR • PUNCTUATION • SENTENCE STRUCTURE

QUESTIONS

Isn't it maddening never to know where to place a comma? You've been writing for 15, 20, 30, or more years, and its correct use still eludes you. Clearly, you're in good company.

FINDING the QUESTIONS

This guide is written for you to keep available so that the answers to all of your basic grammar and punctuation questions are accessible. Finding the answers, however, presupposes questions that are a result of *proofreading.* And, proofreading is simply rereading to make sure you've expressed the ideas as effectively as possible with correct grammar, punctuation, and structure.

Think about the first letter of each of the preceding words: **G** grammar, **P** punctuation, and **S** structure. Together, these letters create GPS; doesn't that combination of letters look familiar? GPS: Global Positioning System. Well, think of proofreading as a system of making sure that the *written words direct the reader to the intended ideas.*

FINDING the ANSWERS

Writing is a process; it doesn't move forward for a sustained period. We write, reread, edit, and write again, reread, edit, and write again;

that's the process. Because we need to review our ideas continuously as we write, without even being aware, we're proofreading along the way. Throughout this book, I'll refer to *proofreading and the questions that it elicits*; that's how we find the answers. And, the answers are here, in this little guide.

The WORD

<table>
<tr><td>Word</td></tr>
<tr><td>Words become meaningful in sentences.</td></tr>
</table>

This guide begins with a discussion about the *word*. Soon after we look at the *word*, we see that it's meaningless until we put it into a sentence. Its place in the sentence, we realize, determines its meaning. Not only does placement determine meaning, but also it determines how the word functions. So, we move into a discussion of the **sentence** and its components.

The SENTENCE

<table>
<tr><td>Function</td></tr>
<tr><td>Placement of a word in a sentence determines its function in the sentence.</td></tr>
</table>

OK, we now have built a sentence by placing words in a certain order. This order reveals, for example, whether the sentence is asking a question or making a command.

There are just *four sentence types.* You know them, perhaps not by name, but through using them; they are in every conversation you have.

<table>
<tr><td>Intention</td></tr>
<tr><td>The purpose of the sentence dictates its type.</td></tr>
</table>

COMBINING SENTENCES

Finally, we think about what we want to communicate. Which ideas do we want to emphasize and which do we want to add just because we want the reader to know a little more information? This leads us into **combining sentences,** and there are four ways to do this. Again, there are not a lot of options;

<table>
<tr><td>Emphasis</td></tr>
<tr><td>Combining of sentences determines the impact of ideas.</td></tr>
</table>

however, each option has specific **punctuation** rules, so we'll work with punctuation through joining sentences to convey our specific intention.

SUMMARY

To sum up, we take a **word** and place it into one of four types of **sentences**; then, we **combine sentences** with appropriate **punctuation**. We continuously **proofread** to confirm our communication. On the next page, you will find an illustration of the preceding information. These are the specific steps to writing effectively. Mastering the mechanics of writing will help you to communicate clearly.

IN CONCLUSION

Once you confirm that your GPS is correct (grammar, punctuation, and structure), you will have an effective piece of writing. The process of writing will no longer be a mystery. When questions arise, you will know exactly where to find the answer. Your skills will improve, and your confidence will grow. It's that simple.

Now, let's move on with "The GPS!"

AN OVERVIEW OF THE MECHANICS OF WRITING

Idea

IDEA

Emphasis
Combining of sentences determines the impact of ideas.

Structures of Sentences

Simple
Compound
Complex
Compound/Complex

IDEA

Intention
The purpose of the sentence dictates its type.

Types of Sentences

Declarative.
Imperative.
Interrogative?
Exclamatory!

IDEA

Function
Placement of a word in a sentence determines its function in the sentence.

Parts of a Sentence

CVS=Complete thought, **V**erb, **S**ubject

Complete thought
Verb/Predicate
Subject
Modifiers
Adjectives
Adverbs
Objects
Subject complements

IDEA

Word
Words become meaningful in sentences

Parts of Speech

A V CAPPIN

Adjective
Verb
Conjunction
Adverb
Pronoun
Preposition
Interjection
Noun

Notes

What we learn with pleasure, we never forget.

—Alfred Mercier

Take time to reflect; proofread.

Chapter 2

Proofreading

Wandering aimlessly through city streets or through lovely neighborhoods and walking lazily in and out of stores are great activities on their own, but if you need to be somewhere at a specific time, you need a plan. And that plan or strategy needs to be clear so that you don't end up going in circles or taking much more time than you anticipated. Today, many people use a **GPS**, Global Positioning System, to assure them of getting to their destination directly and promptly. The **GPS** even asks the drivers if they want to avoid tolls. The **GPS** prepares drivers by giving an overview of the trip, by giving a step-by-step plan, and by announcing turns and shifts in the road. All of these cues assist drivers in arriving at their destinations promptly, safely, and efficiently.

Writing is not different from traveling; writing involves traveling from one idea to another, taking the reader on a journey to a destination of the writer's choice. There are a variety of ways to get there. Some are more effective than others. Of course, writers want to communicate clearly and want to be sure that they guide the reader through the process successfully. Engaging the reader's interest and curiosity is achieved through stylistic choices involving correct **g**rammar, **p**unctuation, and **s**tructure. These elements create *The GPS for Writing*. The writer's **GPS** assures clear communication, which means guiding the reader to an understanding of the writer's purpose.

As you move through the writing process, you naturally reread after every few sentences to confirm that you have been clear. This rereading is called proofreading and involves not only reading for content (logical development of ideas) but also making certain that the elements that assure effective communication are correct. You are confirming the accuracy of your GPS (grammar, punctuation, and structure).

7

Proofreading for Grammar

Proofreading for correct grammar means confirming that, for example, verbs agree with subjects, pronouns agree with antecedents, pronoun case agrees with function, tenses are consistent, and active and passive voice are used correctly. Mastery of these skills is essential for clear communication. (You already know this, or you wouldn't be going through these chapters.) For specific guidance about proofreading for elements of grammar, see the chapters "Words A V CAPPIN" and "Sentence Parts (CVS)."

Proofreading for Punctuation

In the opening sentence of the chapter called "Overview," I ask if you are baffled about placement of commas. Your confusion may come from your not being familiar with the basic rules of comma usage. Here's where it's important to note that rules change. If you're writing in an academic setting, you need to ask which style guide is being followed (Modern Language Association or American Psychological Association or The Chicago Manual of Style). Then, check to see the most recent recommendations by that organization. Some businesses and professions have their own style guides. If your writing is for personal use, this *GPS* will work. The aforementioned guides, including this *GPS,* will help you proofread for your consistent adherence to the accepted rules.

Proofreading for Sentence Structure

As you're proofreading for grammar and punctuation, you will certainly be reading for sentence structure. To know where to place commas, semicolons, and quotation marks, for example, you need to understand the pattern of the sentence you're punctuating. (Refer to the chapter "Sentence Patterns" for more information.)

Proofreading for Spelling

An effective way to proofread for spelling errors is to read from the last word of the sentence back to the first; this will facilitate your focusing on the word without getting caught up in the ideas. Of course, refer to a digital or paper dictionary to confirm the correct homonym (words that sound alike and have different meanings and spellings, such as *their*, *they're*, *there*). This is discussed in "Word Choices."

Proofreading for Logical Development of Ideas

To confirm logical development of ideas, pull out the **topic sentence** (the main-idea sentence) of each paragraph. Read only the topic sentences in all the **body paragraphs**. If these topic sentences move the idea forward logically, if the meaning is clearly developed, then, reading just the topic sentences will reveal the intention of the writing. If the writing is convoluted, illogical, confusing, muddled, then, reading just the topic sentences will reveal where the development of ideas falls apart.

Proofread the **introductory paragraph** to confirm that it gives the reader an idea of what to expect in and from the rest of the reading. Now, read the **concluding paragraph.** Does it echo the introduction? Does it reiterate and restate the writer's intention? Does the **concluding paragraph** leave you with a clear understanding of the purpose of the communication? If the answer to all these questions is yes, then, congratulations! Your writing is logically developed.

Below is an exercise in logical development. The correct order of these sentences takes the reader step-by-step through a process. I hope that these exercises will give you a clear understanding of what is meant by logical development.

LD1 Logical Development—Exercises
(Page 215-216 Answers)

Rearrange these sentences so that they are placed in chronological order. You should be able to make a bed if you follow these sentences when arranged in a logical sequence. You will find answers in Chapter 16. They are arranged in alphabetical order according to the letters identifying the exercise. This exercise is LD1. Check the answers as soon as you complete the work.

1. The bed looks very neat now that I'm finished.

2. The quilt is placed on top of the clean sheets.

3. Ready to place the linens on the bed, I move the bed away from the wall; this allows me to reach around it more easily.

4. I need to get clean sheets and pillowcases from the closet.

5. The bottom sheet needs to be stretched; now, it fits tightly around the corners.

6. Next, I'll push the bed back against the wall.

7. I have to make my bed.

8. The pillows are slipped into the cases.

9. The pillows are placed on top of the cover.

10. The top sheet is placed neatly over the bottom sheet, and the corners are folded and tucked under the mattress.

Being able to arrange ideas in logical order, guided by *The GPS for Writing*, you will get to your destination, which is to effectively communicate ideas.

Notes

The skill of writing is to create a context in which other people can think.

—Edwin Schlossberg

Photo courtesy of Andy Feder

What have we here? Inspiration! Ideas! Words!

Chapter 3

Words (A V CAPPIN)

GRAMMAR • PUNCTUATION • SENTENCE STRUCTURE

Eight Parts of Speech

The names of the parts of speech are fun and easy to learn if you just think and salute **A V CAPPIN!** Just think, "Aye! Aye! Captain!"

A = Adjective
V = Verb
C = Conjunction
A = Adverb
P = Preposition
P = Pronoun
I = Interjection
N = Noun

These words may already be familiar to you, so it's just a matter of putting them, as above, in an order that will be easy for you to remember—just in case you need to remember! So, for me, I just say the letters A, V; then, I say the word CAPPIN! It works for me. Try it!

Now, cover the list above, and see if you can name all eight parts of speech by referring to A V CAPPIN. While reviewing these terms, notice the spelling, especially the two C's in conjunction.

See, you're already *proofreading* by noticing and checking that the spelling is correct. *Proofreading* is the important skill that assures you that you really are writing what you intended. You will get to your destination using *The GPS for Writing.*

ADJECTIVES

Adjective (and Adverb)—These are by far my favorite parts of speech. The language would be utterly boring without these "**A**" words. They add the spice, flavor, and excitement to our language. The "**A**" words are called modifiers, as they modify, describe, and enhance the nouns and verbs we use. Let's discuss the **adjectives** first, as I'd like to follow **A V CAPPIN**.

Look at the following examples of adjectives:

The puppy ran across the street.
> The **tiny**, **black** and **white**, **curly haired** puppy ran swiftly and nervously across the **wide**, **busy** street.

If my example is effective in demonstrating modifiers (adjectives and adverbs), you have a vivid picture of this puppy and his experience.

To go along with **A V CAPPIN**, let's take a moment to discuss adjectives.

The function of an adjective is to give the reader a clear understanding of the nouns and pronouns used in the writing.

Let's work on this sentence. **I have a puppy.**

What kind of puppy?
> a tiny puppy
> a black and white puppy
> a curly haired puppy
> a plump puppy
> a frisky puppy
> a friendly puppy

I'll bet you can think of more adjectives to describe this puppy. Think about the puppy's eyes and the puppy's tail. Words that you would choose to describe the puppy's eyes and tail are adjectives.

Note that I started with the question, "**What kind of** puppy?"

Adjectives always answer the question, "**What kind of?**"
What kind of puppy would you like?
>I would like a friendly, long-haired, frisky puppy.

How many puppies did you see?
>I saw **two** puppies.

How much do you think the puppy weighs?
>I think the puppy weighs **twenty-five** pounds.

Which one of the puppies would you like?
>I would like the **spotted**, **black** and **white** puppy.

The four questions to locate adjectives in a sentence are illustrated above.
What kind of?
How many?
How much?
Which one?

Forms of Adjectives

As we move through this grammar guide, you will see that **words, phrases, and clauses may function as adjectives** in sentences. Therefore, several words in one sentence may be adjectives.

There's a grammatical structure called **verbals.** These are words that we generally recognize as verbs; however, as verbals, they do not function as verbs. The verbals are called infinitives, participles, and gerunds. Participles and infinitives act as adjectives in sentences. (We'll discuss gerunds in the "noun" section.) Is this confusing? Well, read on, and let's see if we can clarify this.

Present participles end in *ing*. **Running** water is always cool. **Running** is a verb form used as an adjective. It's describing "water." **Past participles** usually end in **d** or **ed**. **Burned** toast is very crunchy. **Burned** is a verb form used to describe "toast"; it's used as an adjective.

Infinitive used as an adjective.
The model had cosmetics **to spare**. The infinitive **to spare** is describing "cosmetics." Since "cosmetics" is a noun, words that modify it are adjectives. **To spare** is an infinitive acting as an adjective.

Prepositional phrases can be used as adjectives.
The woman **in the yellow, silk dress** is my dance teacher. **In the yellow, silk dress** is describing "woman," which is a noun. Adjectives describe nouns.

(By the way, an important mission of this book is to help you develop the vocabulary of grammar, punctuation, and sentence structure. You don't have to read this book in any order. Just skip around the text, and look at the information as needed.)

A1 Adjectives—Exercises
(Page 207 Answers)

Identify the thirty-four adjectives in the following sentences. You are looking for words that are functioning as adjectives in these sentences, that is, all the words that are modifying nouns (tip → include words sometimes called articles—a, an, the).

1. I am a loyal baseball fan, but my team is really awful this year!

2. The dedicated coach is doing all he can do.

3. The players are serious fighters and have team spirit, but nothing seems to help.

4. The players are very young, but I'm not sure that's a good excuse.

5. They don't seem to have the skill needed to be national champions.

6. Maybe it's their training that's at fault; I really don't know.

7. Too many good players are injured, and others seem to just throw the ball away.

8. What I do know is that I am really hurt and disappointed by careless players and rude fans.

9. However, I will always be an avid baseball fan through good times and bad times.

10. I look forward to next season when I know (like a true baseball fan) that my team will be the champion once again!

Photo courtesy of Andy Feder

The magic is in the detail.

VERBS

If I were to ask you to define a **verb**, I'll bet you would say, "An action word." You'd feel quite confident in that definition. OK, I'll concede; verbs tell action.

Nicki's horse gracefully **jumped** over the log.

In the hopes of winning a first-place ribbon, Lori **created** a magnificent window box of brilliantly colored, summer flowers.

Yes, your definition works well in the sentences above.
But, let me ask you; can you as easily and confidently identify the verbs in the sentences that follow?

I am a very strong swimmer.
Which word is the verb?

This chocolate, mocha-chip ice cream is the best!
Which word is the verb?

OK, I will offer you a definition of a verb that will always, yes, always, help you find the verb. Here's the question to ask: What is the tense in the sentence? Tense means time; is the sentence talking about now (present tense), yesterday (past tense), or tomorrow (future tense)?

I **am** a very strong swimmer. What is the tense in this sentence?
If you don't know the answer, here's another question: Can you change this sentence to make it another time, such as yesterday (past), today (present), tomorrow (future)? OK, let's make it yesterday.

I **was** a very strong swimmer.

Rewrite the sentence above to make it occur tomorrow. Change the tense from past to future.

I **will be** a very strong swimmer. Now, you have future tense, **will be**.

There you go. The words that you changed to alter the tense/time are the verbs. Get it?

Let's try again.

Nicki's horse gracefully **jumped** over the log.
What's the tense?
Nicki's horse **jumps** gracefully over the log.
Nicki's horse **will jump** gracefully over the log.

Do the restatements of the original sentence help you identify the verb(s)? The verbs are **jumped,** past tense; **jumps**, present tense; **will jump**, future tense.

As you see, verbs may be more than one word. Sometimes a second word is needed to help the main verb.

To create the future tense, the verb **will** is used.
Will is called a helping verb; some call it an auxiliary verb.

Helping verbs, also known as **auxiliary verbs**, have an important function: to tell the tense of the main verb.

In the sentence, "The horse **jumps** gracefully," the verb is **jumps** (present tense).
If we want to change the tense to future, we need to add a helping verb. The horse **will jump**.
If we want to change the tense again to indicate that the horse jumped before he won the contest, we would write, "The horse **had jumped** the fence before he **won** the contest." So, we have two different verbs in the preceding sentence. **Had jumped** is the past perfect, and **won** is the past. (The past perfect tense is defined in a few paragraphs; read on.)

The following list includes **helping verbs**—auxiliary verbs.
If you read down each column, I'll bet that you can memorize these helping verbs in no time. Try it!

Have	Can	May	Shall	Will
Has	Could	Might	Should	Would
Had		Must		

The horse **will jump**.
Jump tells what the horse is doing.
Will tells when the horse will do it.

Consequently, both words are needed to identify what was done and when it was done. And, that's what the verb does; the verb tells **when** something is done. The **verb** indicates **tense,** which is another word for **time.** If you have trouble identifying the verb, ask yourself **when** the subject did the action.

Let's review this. If you still can't find the verb, change the tense/time of the sentence. I believe that you will know how to do this without really thinking about it. The word that will change the tense/time is the verb.

Simple Tenses

Sam **studies** every day after classes.   Simple present tense
OK, which word is the verb? Which word can you change to reflect the tense (time) of what Sam is doing? Can you make the tense reflect yesterday or tomorrow?

Sam **studied**. (yesterday)   Simple past tense
Sam **will study**. (tomorrow)   Simple future tense

As you have seen, the **verb** tells **when** the action occurred.

Now, let's consider a time line to illustrate **tense**.

←Past_____Present_____→Future→

←Yesterday_____Today_____→Tomorrow→

←(you)Baby_____Adult_____→ RIP (Rest in Peace!)

Photo courtesy of Andy Feder

Look at the graceful tree. The limbs were bare in the winter. In the spring, the leaves appeared. In the summer, the leaves were green; then, they became red. Now, they are gold. Soon, they will be gone, again, as the cycle resumes. (Look at the tenses in the sentences.)

Perfect Tenses

As you know, not everything occurs exactly at a particular time in the past. There are times when we need to indicate that an action was completed before another specific time or action.

Sometimes things occur in the recent past, such as this morning. There are times when we want to express that things occurred in the distant past, such as when my grandfather was a child. And, sometimes things have not yet occurred and will occur soon. Additionally, perfect tenses may indicate that an action was begun in the past and continued into the present.

Perfect tenses are introduced by the helping verbs **had**, **have/has**, and **will have**. (Helping verbs are also known as auxiliary verbs.)

You have just read definitions of **Perfect Tenses**: Past Perfect, Present Perfect, and Future Perfect.

1. The past perfect tense uses the word "had" and indicates an action that was completed before another past action.
    Marilyn **had loved** her husband before he was in college.

2. The present perfect tense uses the word "has/have" and indicates an action that began in the past and is linked to the present, and an action completed in the recent indefinite past.
    Marilyn **has loved** her husband since they were in college.

3. The future perfect tense uses the words "will have" and indicates an action that will be completed before another future action.
    Marilyn **will have loved** her husband for thirty years when they celebrate their 50th college reunion next year.

Perfect tenses help the writer show that **one action occurred before or after another** action. For example, "She testified that she had seen him commit a crime." *Testified* is past tense (recent past) and *had seen* is past perfect tense (distant past).

To create **Perfect Tenses**, always use a form of the word **have**. With the word **have,** only use the **past participle** of the verb, which is the form of the verb ending in **ed** or **n** and, sometimes **t**. Examples of this are jumped, written, and burnt.

The Perfect Tenses would fall on these places in the time line.

←Past Perf.	Past	Pres.Perf.	Present	Future Perf.	Future→

had jumped   jumped   have jumped   jump(s)   will have jumped   will jump

has jumped

We have discussed six tenses: two past, two present, and two future. There are more. As in other languages, verbs are quite complicated. (In fact, as you'll see later in this guide, the verb is the only part of speech that can stand alone as a sentence.)

Progressive Tenses

How do we indicate that an action takes time to complete, that it is a continuing action? The **progressive tense** is used to indicate **continuing action**. The main verb in the **progressive tenses** is introduced by the words **was/were**, **is**, and **will be**.

> Imagine a very large, old tree with thick, strong, and very deep roots. Well, here comes a violent storm, and it whips around everything in its path, including this gnarly, old tree. The tree doesn't just fall; it rocks back and forth slowly, tearing at its roots as it gives in to the unyielding winds until the tree, finally, wrests free from its hold on the earth and begins the agonizing process of falling.

How would you indicate this **continuing action** of the old tree? We know that the act of falling took time, as the tree rocked and rocked. So, here's how it's done.

Focus on the form of the verb **to sway** (which means to rock).

1. Once the storm hits, the tree **will be swaying** from the force of the treacherous winds.

2. As the storm hits, the tree **is swaying**.

3. As the storm left our area, the tree **was swaying** from the force of the winds until it finally fell.

This form of the verb is the **progressive form** and has three parts: future progressive, present progressive, past progressive, as illustrated above. As we discussed, some actions take time to complete; we convey the sustained time by using a form of the verb **to be** plus the **ing** form of the main verb.

Perfect Progressive Tenses

This is a combination of the perfect tense and the progressive tense. The perfect progressive tenses include past perfect progressive, present perfect progressive, and future perfect progressive. The words used to help create these tenses, the auxiliary verbs, are **had been**, **have been/has been**, and **will have been**.

Let's see what happens to a verb as we take it through the twelve tenses.

Regular Verbs

To walk is a regular verb; the core spelling of the word remains the same. To indicate the past tense of regular verbs, add **ed**, **t**, or **en.** Note the letters at the end of the verb "to walk" as it changes tenses.

TENSES

When the verb changes within the tense, the additional form is given.

To walk
Past	I walked	
Past perfect	I had walked	
Past progressive	I was/we were walking	
Past perfect progressive	I had been walking	
Present	I walk	he/she/it walks
Present perfect	I have walked	he/she/it has walked
Present progressive	I am walking	he/she/it is walking
Present perfect progressive	I have been walking	he/she/it has been walking
Future	I will walk	
Future perfect	I will have walked	
Future progressive	I will be walking	
Future perfect progressive	I will have been walking	

It's your turn to take the regular verb **to kiss** through the twelve tenses. Check the answer page, and refer to the chart above as needed. (Note that in the present tense, an **s** is added to the verb following he/she/it, which is the third person singular form. This will be the next topic discussed: conjugation of verbs.)

Irregular Verbs

Now, look at an irregular verb. The helping (auxiliary) verbs remain the same. The main verb goes through many changes that a regular verb does not. Here is an example of the verb **to go** taken through all of its tenses.

To go

Past	I went
Past perfect	I had gone
Past progressive	I was/we were going
Past perfect progressive	I had been going
Present	I go
Present perfect	I have gone/she has gone
Present progressive	I am going/she is going
Present perfect progressive	I have been going/she has been going
Future	I will go
Future perfect	I will have gone.
Future progressive	I will be going
Future perfect progressive	I will have been going

Perfect tenses = to have+participle

Progressive tenses = to be+verb+ing

Emphatic forms of the verb begin with a form of "to be."
    Present emphatic form
        I do exercise daily.
        She does exercise daily.
    Past emphatic form
        I did exercise daily.

Let's see you take the irregular verb **to do** through the twelve tenses. Check the answers at the end of this guide, and refer to the chart above as needed.

(Notice that the verbs are identified as "to do" not just "do." When studying grammar, we discuss verbs in their *infinitive* form, which includes the word "to.")

Note: For lists of regular and irregular **verb forms**, consult comprehensive grammar sites such as OWL.com

Conjugating Verbs

You may be wondering why the pronouns, **I, he, she, it** are repeated in the listing of tenses. Well, here's the story:

In English, all verbs go through what's called **conjugation**. This is the process of considering the verb with one person (singular) or with many people (plural).

We look at verbs from the point of who's doing it. Am **I** doing it? Am I saying that **you** are doing it? Am I writing about **him** or **her** or **it** doing something? I can also write about my doing it with other people.

Let's substitute **dance** for **it**. Am I dancing? Am I referring to you or him or her or it (a puppy) dancing? Am I including myself in a group dancing? Am I talking about another group dancing?

If **I** am dancing, that's called 1st-person **singular**. I am referring to myself; that involves one person.

If I say you are dancing, we are, now, two people, and you are the **2nd person**.

If I say he, she, or it is dancing, I'm not referring to you. I'm referring to him, her, it, and that's called **3rd person**.

If I include myself in a group of people, that's called the first-person plural. **We** is 1st person, again, because it includes me, along with other people.

If I want to directly address a group of people, I would use the word **you**, again, but this time it would mean more than one person; it's 2nd-person plural. (Talking to my class, I would say, "How are **you** today?" In this sentence, **you** refers to many people.)

Finally, if I wanted to refer to a group on the dance floor far across the room, I would use the word **they**, and that's known as 3rd-person plural.

In chart form, conjugation would look like this.

Chart for Conjugating Verbs

	Singular	Plural
First person	I	we
Second person	you	you
Third person	he, she, it	they

I'll include a verb in the present tense to illustrate.

Conjugation of "To Walk" in the Present Tense

	Singular	Plural
First person	I walk	we walk
Second person	you walk	you walk
Third person	he, she, it walks	they walk

V3 Verb Tenses—Exercise
(Page 229 Answers)

Let's see if you can conjugate the verb **to look** in the present tense.

The third-person singular in the present tense always ends in s. Whether conjugating a regular or irregular verb in the **present tense**, the **third**-person singular **always** ends with an **s**.

Check the answer page to make certain that you are correct.

(Not every sentence has an error. Sixteen changes need to be made.)
For consistency, stay with the tense reflected in the first sentence.

1. There once is a dog names Tucker.

2. He is found as a puppy in the East Village of New York City several years ago.

3. Nobody wants him except one person who takes him home even though she had two other dogs at that time.

4. Within several years, he grows up to be a beautiful black dog with silky fur.

5. When he is a puppy, he loves the water and could swim long distances.

6. When he was a frisky puppy, he often jumps into a canoe or swims along side it.

7. He also will love to fetch sticks and go after tennis balls thrown into the water.

8. When he was a little dog, he disappears into the woods around the water and would be gone for close to an hour.

9. Our guess was that he will be probably chasing an animal.

10. Tucker is fearless in nature but will be afraid of brooms and people's feet.

11. He lives a long life.

Review the underlined verbs in the following sentences. Notice that the author is referring to a storm that already happened and caused damage. Keep all of the verbs in the past tense: simple past, past perfect, past progressive, or past perfect progressive.

Hurricane Sandy by Amer Yahia

1. On October 22, 2012, the hurricane known as Sandy <u>floods</u> New York City, New Jersey, and other parts of Pennsylvania.

2. Properties <u>are damage</u> due to Sandy.

3. Many people <u>will lose</u> their homes.

4. The people <u>are placed</u> in temporary shelters.

5. The government <u>has</u> to pay fifty-four billion dollars to aid the Sandy storm victims.

6. There <u>are</u> at least 149 people <u>confirmed</u> dead including all states.

7. The subways <u>are</u> flooded and <u>will be closing</u>.

8. Airlines services <u>will have been cancelled</u>.

9. Mayor Bloomberg <u>has been closing</u> most of the gas stations in New York City and New Jersey.

10. After all that, President Barack Obama <u>gathers</u> with New Jersey Governor Chris Christie to go over the aftermath of the hurricane.

Other Facts About Verbs

Transitive and **intransitive** verbs must be discussed; however, because their important function is joining parts of a sentence, that's exactly where they will be discussed. To read about transitive and intransitive verbs, go to Chapter 4, "Sentence Parts."

Mood and voice will also be discussed in Chapter 4, "Sentence Parts."

CONJUNCTIONS

Now, you say, if I have all these ideas and all these words, how do I join them to get my writing to flow? The answer is to use conjunctions because they help us glide from one idea to another.

Let's look at conjunctions; then, we will discuss them in detail.

There are four types of conjunctions. (Some grammarians discuss conjunctive adverbs with **adverbs** not with conjunctions.)

1. **Coordinating conjunctions** are used to join grammatically similar words or word groups.
   The seven coordinating conjunctions are **and, but, so, or, for, nor, yet**.
   The first letter of these words creates the phrase **ABS OF NY**. Does this help you to remember these conjunctions?

   I like you, **and** you like me. (Two independent clauses, two sentences, are joined with a coordinating conjunction.)

2. **Conjunctive adverbs** are similar to coordinating conjunctions as they also join sentences. These joining words indicate how sentences (independent clauses) relate to each other. Conjunctive adverbs are preceded by a semicolon and followed by a comma.

   Included in the list of these conjunctions are "furthermore, indeed, therefore, consequently, however, moreover, in fact, nevertheless, then." The first letter of these words creates the (made up) word **FITCHMINT**. Does that help you to remember conjunctive adverbs?

   Teaching is a glorious profession; therefore, I will teach forever!

   See how the clauses relate to each other? More discussion of **conjunctive adverbs** and how they create sentence variety is in "Sentence Patterns."

3. **Correlative conjunctions** are used to join similar elements of the sentence, and they always come in pairs.

   These conjunctions are "neither/nor, either/or, both/and, not/but, both/and, not only/but also."

   Neither Neil **nor** Nafti wanted to walk the dogs in the rain.

4. **Subordinating conjunctions** are used to join clauses (a group of words that include a subject and a verb). Because introducing a clause with a subordinating conjunction makes it a dependent clause, meaning it can't stand alone as a sentence, its meaning becomes less important than the independent clause it relies on to create a grammatically correct sentence.

   These conjunctions include **when, although, because, if, that,** and **since**. The first letter of each of these words creates the (fun) word **WABITS**. Does that help you to remember subordinating conjunctions?

   Because you are a crazy and wild dancer, I'll go to the party with you.
   I'll go to the party with you because you are a crazy and wild dancer. (The comma after "you" is not required before a subordinate conjunction that introduces a dependent clause.)

The purpose of a conjunction is to join words, phrases, and clauses. If all the sentences we write are short, the writing will be boring, and the ideas will feel choppy. Sometimes, we want to join ideas to help the writing flow. Writers need to be aware of the construction of their sentences to make certain the writing is interesting to the reader. This is discussed in detail in the chapter "Sentence Patterns."

ADVERBS

Take a close look at the word ad**verb**. Note the word "verb" is in ad**verb**? Well, that's a way to remember that ad**verb**s describe or modify **verbs.** In other words, adverbs add to verbs. Now, doesn't that help you to remember what adverbs do in sentences? Additionally, most adverbs end in **ly**.

Sometimes, adverbs are created by adding **ly** to adjectives.

The **quick** horse ran home.   adjective
The horse ran **quickly** home.   adverb

The **impatient** baby screamed for the bottle.   adjective
The baby screamed **impatiently** for the bottle. adverb

The trusted way to find adverbs is to ask these questions: When? How? Where?

Adverbs modify verbs, adjectives, and other adverbs. (In the chapter on sentence diagramming, you will see how adverbs function as modifiers of verbs, adjectives, and other adverbs.)

Here's an example of an adverb modifying a verb:

The fat hen **proudly** laid a big, round egg.
How did she lay the egg? See the word **how**? The answer is **proudly**; that's the adverb because it's telling **how** she laid the egg.

Here's an example of an adverb modifying an adjective:

The fat hen proudly laid a **very** big and **perfectly** round egg.
The words **very** and **perfectly** answer **how** big was the egg. The egg was very big.
How round was the egg. The egg was perfectly round.
Words that answer **how** are adverbs. Here we have the adverbs **very** and **perfectly** modifying the adjectives **big** and **round**.

Here's an example of an adverb modifying an adverb:

The fat hen **very** proudly laid a very big and perfectly round egg.
How proudly did she lay the egg? She laid it very proudly.
Very answers the question **how**.
Very is an adverb modifying another adverb, which is **proudly**.

How round was the egg?
The egg was **very** round.
Very is an adverb modifying the adjective **round**.

The hen laid the egg first and then strutted around the yard.
When did she lay the egg? She laid it *first*.
When did she strut? She strutted *then*.

PREPOSITIONS

Prepositions are modifiers, and they always exist in phrases. A phrase is a group of related words. The prepositional phrase always begins with a preposition and ends with a noun or pronoun. This noun or pronoun is called the object of the preposition. (Objects answer the questions what or whom.)

Find the object of the preposition in the sentence below. Take the preposition and ask what or whom. The answer will be the object of the preposition. If the object is a pronoun, be sure to use an objective-case pronoun.

After tutoring my classmates, I felt like a professor.
After (← preposition) tutoring my classmates (← object of preposition),
I felt like (← preposition) a professor (← object of preposition).

Prepositional phrases show the relationship between nouns and verbs and their modifiers.
By means near to or next to
For means purpose
At, before, after, on show time or place
Like, **as** show comparison
After, before, on show time
Of shows possession
To, through, toward show direction

I want a home **by a lake**.
I'm going to the store **for apples**.

Prepositional phrases act as modifiers, adjectives and adverbs and will be discussed. Because prepositional phrases function as adjectives and adverbs, which are not vital to the basic structure of a sentence, the subject and verb of a sentence will never be in a prepositional phrase.

The nine most commonly used prepositions are stated here. Familiarizing yourself with these words will help you to spot prepositional phrases.

The Nine Most Commonly Used Prepositions

at	from	on
by	in	to
for	of	with

The bird flew **to** the tree **with** a worm **in** her beak.
to the tree **To** is the preposition, and **tree** is the noun that is functioning as the object of the preposition.

with a worm **With** is the preposition, and **worm** is the object of the preposition.

in her beak **In** is the preposition, and **beak** is the object of the preposition.

Some grammar books and some grammarians say that a sentence should never end with a preposition. Other reliable and respected sources indicate that a sentence may end with a preposition when the words seem to flow better.

Example:
Having fully recovered from the nearly fatal accident, the woman had much to be thankful **for.**

To rework this sentence would be awkward.
Having fully recovered from the nearly fatal accident, the woman had much for which to be thankful.

However, to conform to the rules of standard English, if possible, do not end a sentence with a preposition.

PRONOUNS

Pronouns take the place of nouns in sentences. For example, "**it**" would be the pronoun for "car." (Pronoun cases are discussed in "Sentence Parts." Gender-neutral pronouns are discussed in "Gender-Neutral Language" in the chapter "Word Choices.")

The car (noun) is a Toyota (noun).
It (pronoun) is a good car, and I (pronoun) enjoy the comfort and ease of driving it.

Indefinite Personal Pronouns are Singular and Plural

Singular indefinite pronouns refer to singular nouns. Think of these as the **body** and **one** pronouns; they are **singular** pronouns, yes, singular. (See the discussion of these pronouns in "Gender-Neutral Language" in the chapter "Word Choices.")

anybody	nobody	somebody	everybody
anyone	no one	someone	everyone

Did **somebody** forget her (not their) umbrella in the store? (This example conforms to the standard rule of agreement of pronoun with antecedent. The antecedent is the word to which the pronoun refers, and, according to standard English, the pronoun reflects the singular or plural quality of the noun.)

If these pronouns function as the subject of a sentence or clause, they are followed by singular verbs.
Did **anyone see** his umbrella?
Everyone is present in class today.
I think that **somebody has** a question.

Plural Indefinite Pronouns refer to plural nouns:
Both
Few
Many
Several

Other Pronoun Facts

1. **Identify yourself last.**
   When a sentence is about you and someone else, always place yourself last.
   Would you like to go to the poetry reading with Tómas, Mária, and me?

2. **Check for correct choice of pronoun case. (Pages 58-59, Cases of Pronouns)**
   If you're not sure which pronoun to use, drop the other person's name or pronoun and see which sounds right.
   She/her and I/me walked with he/him.
   She walked with him.
   I walked with him.
   She and I walked with him.

3. **Apostrophes and pronouns don't go together.**
   Possessive pronouns **never** have an apostrophe. When you look at the list below, you will see that you already know that rule.
   My, mine
   Your, yours
   His, her, hers, its
   Our, ours
   Their, theirs

   See, no apostrophes, yet each of these words expresses ownership.

   Indefinite pronouns—the "bodies" and the "ones"—take an apostrophe when possessive.
   anybody
   nobody
   somebody
   everybody
   anyone
   no one
   someone
   everyone

   That must be somebody's book on the floor in the lounge.

4. For a discussion of gender-neutral language, specifically pronouns, see the chapter "Word Choices."

INTERJECTIONS

These are words that express strong emotion and are followed by an exclamation mark.

Yikes!
Ouch!
Oops!

Sometimes interjections are imitations of the sound emitted by the word referenced.

Whack!

Mimicking the sound will create more effective writing than explaining the sound to the reader.

When the tennis player slammed the ball, the **whack** echoed throughout the stadium.

NOUNS

A noun is the name of a person (Rashid), a place (New York City), a thing (film), and an idea (a dream). Nouns are generally preceded by one of the words *a, an*, or *the*; these words may also be called noun pointers.

Nouns can be singular (bird) and plural (birds). Nouns function in sentences as subjects and objects.

There are **proper nouns**, which are always capitalized (President Obama), and common nouns, which are not capitalized (the president of the country).

Nouns can own things, which means nouns can show possession. A possessive apostrophe may be added to a noun: my professor's computer.

A **count noun** names things that are countable, such as cookies.
There are more than twenty-four cookies in the container.

Fewer is an adjective used with count nouns.
We will have fewer cookies to sell if you leave them with me.

A **noncount noun** names things that cannot be counted, such as milk.
We have too much milk in the pitcher to carry it safely to the porch.

Less is an adjective used with noncount nouns.
   We have less energy after running the marathon.

Collective nouns can be singular or plural. If considering a group as one entity, the noun is singular. If referring to the individuals within the group, the noun is considered plural. *Family, flock, senate,* and *jury* are examples of collective nouns.

My *family is* gathering in Jamaica, West Indies for the holidays.
       (singular—family as one)
My *family are* taking separate vacations this summer.
       (plural—members of the family)

The *jury is* deadlocked.
       (singular—the jury as one)
The *jury are* arguing among themselves.
       (plural—members of the jury)

The *family are* in disagreement over the sale of their company to an outsider.
       (plural—members of the family)
The *family is* in disagreement over the sale of its company to an outsider.
       (singular—family as one)

Please note...

Verbals are mentioned in this chapter because they function as adjectives, adverbs, and nouns. The three kinds of verbals are gerunds, infinitives, and participles.

Infinitives generally begin with the word "to" and function as adjectives, adverbs, and nouns. In sentences, they could function as a subject, object, or modifier.

Gerunds are forms of verbs that act as nouns. **Gerunds** end with "ing." They function in sentences as subjects and objects.

Participles are verbals that function as adjectives; therefore, in sentences, they are modifiers.

Verbals will be discussed in the chapter "Sentence Parts."

Identify the part of speech of the italicized words in the following sentences. Check the answers at the end of this guide to confirm your understanding.

1. Briana bought *cut* flowers for her birthday.

2. The florist actually *cut* the flowers while Briana was watching.

3. Unfortunately, one of the florists had a deep *cut* from the thorns on the roses.

4. Women, it seems more than men, *long* for flowers on their birthdays.

5. Exotic flowers with *long* stems are most expensive.

6. I love having lots of *plants* in my home.

7. After the summer, my sister *plants* her flowers in her backyard.

8. I have plenty of *light* in my apartment, so my flowers are happy.

9. I keep the plants in *light* containers, so I can move them around easily.

10. Briana *will light* the candles and put the candles and the flowers on the table.

Helpful Web Sites

Adjectives and Adverbs
http://www.youtube.com/watch?v=mYzGLzFuwxI

Conjunction
www.youtube.com/watch?v=mkO87mkgcNo

Grammar Worksheets
http://www.superteacherworksheets.com

Notes

There is music in words, and it can be heard, you know, by thinking.
—E.L. Doctorow

Notes

Speak properly and in as few words as you can but always plainly; the end of speech is not ostentation but to be understood.

—William Penn

Compelling writing, like an intriguing landscape, includes a variety of structures.

Chapter 4

Sentence Parts (CVS)

Now that you have looked at words in isolation—not in sentences—and understand that their meaning and function are clear only in sentences, let's see how to construct sentences and proofread them for correct grammar, which involves placement of words in sentences.

I'm going to identify parts of a sentence, but don't worry about memorizing them or expecting them to make complete sense until we look at the whole sentence. There are specific questions that will help you to identify the parts of sentences.

However, before we move into the chapter, let me explain why I have written CVS in the title. As you read through the next few pages and the discussion of parts of a sentence, you'll learn that to be a sentence, a group of words must create a **C**omplete thought and contain a **V**erb and a **S**ubject. These three components are essential to form a sentence, **CVS**. That's why **CVS** is included in the title of this chapter.

C Complete Thought

Let's start with the C, which represents a complete thought. When you string several words together, you can *feel* if the idea expressed in those words is complete

Try it. Say, "because I am thirsty." Does that feel complete? Don't be concerned about grammar, at the moment. Just think; do these four words express a full thought?

How about this: "I am thirsty." Does this group of words feel complete?

Listen to your voice when you say this string of words: because I am thirsty. If your voice seems to settle after you read the words, it's likely that the words create a sentence. If you feel more words are needed, it's likely that the string of words is not a sentence.

As you work through these exercises, you will begin to understand what is meant by complete. You will learn that a string of words cannot be a sentence unless it has a verb, a subject, and a complete thought.

V Verb

A **verb** indicates time (past, present, future) and may also tell what the subject is doing. As the most important part of the sentence, the verb has many fascinating and complex properties. We discussed some in "Words," and we will discuss more here.

Every sentence expresses time or tense. Let's check for the tense. Without knowing the tense, you can find the verb by identifying the words that will change this sentence from present to past or past to future. Let's see.

Examples:
William Shakespeare's play *Hamlet* evokes intense emotion from the students.
Ok, now change the time/tense.

William Shakespeare's play *Hamlet* will evoke intense emotion from the students.

You see? Changing the form of the word *evokes* to *will evoke* changes the time/tense of the sentence. The verb's job is to tell the time/tense in the sentence. (Another word for verb is **predicate**.)

To find the verb, ask yourself, "What is the subject doing? What is the tense/time of the sentence (past, present, future)? Which word or words can change the tense of the sentence?"

As in the sentence, **William Shakespeare's play** *Hamlet* **evokes intense emotion from the students,** we see that the word *evokes* can be changed to the past tense, **evoked**, and to the future tense, **will evoke**. You see, the word in the sentence that can be changed to reflect other tenses is the verb.

As discussed in Chapter 3, some verbs require **helping verbs** (also known as auxiliary verbs). These words are important parts of the verb because they suggest the tense when they are added onto the main verb (which is usually the verb that tells the action). Together, they create a **verb phrase**.

The most common helping verbs are:

have	can	may	shall	will
has	could	might	should	would
had		must		

You already use these verb phrases (word groups) in daily conversations. Here's an example:

I **have watched** that show every night this week.

   The verb phrase is **have watched**.

Students **should work** consistently.

   The verb phrase is **should work**.

Transitive and intransitive verbs were mentioned in Chapter 3. Let's go into detail at this point because they are responsible for two parts of the sentence that will be discussed in this chapter.

Transitive verbs send action to a receiver, and that receiver is called the direct object. To find the **direct object**, say the verb, and, then, say *who* or *what*. (*Objects* are discussed, again, after *subjects*.)

For example, Shakepeare wrote *Romeo and Juliet.*

What did Shakespeare write?

Shakespeare wrote what?

Shakespeare wrote *Romeo and Juliet.*

The verb that sends action is transitive: **wrote**.

The word(s) that receives that action is called the direct object: *Romeo and Juliet.*

Transitive verbs are also responsible for **indirect objects;** they are placed between the transitive verb and the direct object. To find the indirect object, say the verb; then, say *to whom* or *for whom*.

Here's an example of an indirect object and a direct object:
Janet baked Dimitri a birthday cake.
Find the direct object—Janet baked *what*? Cake
Find the indirect object—Janet baked *for whom*? Dimitri

Clearly, Janet didn't bake Dimitri; she baked a cake.
Got it?

Intransitive verbs do not send action. Some intransitive verbs are followed by modifiers of single words, phrases, or clauses. Other intransitive verbs "link" or join the subject part of the sentence with the predicate part.
(The predicate part of the sentence includes the verb and all the words that come after the verb. This is an **intransitive linking verb**.)

The subject complement follows an intransitive linking verb and can be a noun, pronoun, or adjective. The subject complement (completer) refers back to the subject by describing it or renaming it. (Subject completers are discussed, again, in more detail, in paragraphs below.)

I sleep well near the ocean. Do you, too?
In the sentence above, the verb *sleep* is followed by an adverb, *well*, not a direct object or a subject completer. *Sleep* is an intransitive verb.

The birthday cake is chocolate.
There's no "action" in this sentence. *Is* does not send action. It tells time/tense as all verbs do.
The word *chocolate* is describing the subject. *Chocolate* is an adjective describing the subject; it is a **subject complement**.

In the sentence above, the verb *is* links or joins the subject part of the sentence, *The birthday cake*, with the predicate part of the sentence *is chocolate*. The **intransitive verb** that we are discussing here is a **linking verb**, for it links the subject part of the sentence with the subject complement.

Because these two sides of the sentence rename and refer to each other, they can be reversed, that is, the subject complement can become the subject of the sentence, and the subject can become the predicate part of the sentence. Consequently, if the pronoun is the subject complement, the subject case pronoun must be used. Let's look at this.

Some people, especially English teachers, say, "The teacher is I." Did that ever confuse you? Or they may say, "The outstanding student is she." Do you, therefore, wonder why the pronouns "I" and "she" are used?

Consider the following examples:
The professor is I.
Professor is the subject; *I* is the subject complement.
Is, we determined, is a linking verb because it links the subject with the subject complement. It does not tell or show action, so it does not take a direct object.

If we were to turn the sentence around, it would be, "I am the professor."

The champion basketball players are they.
Turn the sentence around so that the subject becomes the subject complement.
They are the champion basketball players.
Are links the two parts of the sentence. Therefore, a subjective, or nominative case pronoun, must be used after an **intransitive linking verb**. (Pronoun cases are discussed later in this chapter under *Putting Sentence Parts Together.*)

René Descartes, the French philosopher, said, "I think; therefore, I am." Neither *think* nor *am* has an object or subject complement; therefore, both verbs are intransitive.

S Subject

A **subject** is a noun or pronoun that names *who* or *what* the sentence is about. The subject may also answer *who* or *what* is doing the action.

The simple subject is the main idea of the sentence, the noun or pronoun without its modifiers. The complete subject includes the simple subject and all its word or word-group modifiers.

The very popular valedictorian of our graduating class attended the top university in the country.
The simple subject is *valedictorian*.
The complete subject is *"The very popular valedictorian of our graduating class."*

Objects

An **object** is a word that completes the meaning of transitive verbs, prepositional phrases, and infinitives. "Objects" are always nouns and objective-case pronouns.

Direct objects answer the questions *whom* and *what*.
Take the verb/predicate and ask verb + what or whom.

Ray threw the ball. Ray threw what? The answer is the **direct object**, *ball*.

Sam loves *to dance*. (**Infinitive** functioning as direct object)
Infinitives are verb forms, too. They generally include the word "to" plus the verb. In the sentence above, *to dance* is the infinitive; it's naming what Sam loves; it's a verb form used as a noun and functioning as the direct object in the sentence. The word that tells us the tense is *loves*, so *loves* is the verb.

Sam loves *dancing*. (**Gerund** functioning as a direct object)
Dancing is naming an action. *Dancing* does not tell us the tense; therefore, it's not a verb. Because it names an activity, it is a noun. Actually, it's a **gerund**, because is a verb form used as a noun and functioning as a direct object in this sentence.

Indirect objects answer the questions *to whom* and *for whom*.
Ray threw Harry the ball. Ray threw to whom? The answer is the **indirect object**, *Harry*.

Objects of prepositions are at the end of the prepositional phrase and complete the meaning of the prepositional phrase.
The fluffy bird flew up the tree. The bird flew up what? The **object of the preposition** is *tree*.

Objects of infinitives, again, complete the meaning of the infinitive and answer the questions *what* or *whom*.
The professor asked Tonya to take Maurice and Mária to the advisement center.
The infinitive is *to take*, and the objects are *Maurice* and *Mária*.

Objects of gerunds complete the meaning of the gerund. Gerunds are forms of verbs, so they can have objects.

I don't like drinking tea.
Drinking is the gerund; ***tea*** is its object.

Passing her exams is foremost on her mind this semester.
Passing is the gerund: ***exams*** is the object.

Rejecting any job offer these days is a big mistake.
Rejecting is the gerund, and ***job*** is the object of the gerund.

Photo © SVLuma, 2011. Used under license from Shutterstock, Inc.

Linking verbs, like bridges, join things.

Subject Complements

A **subject complement** (also called subject completer) follows *intransitive linking verbs* and describes or renames the subject. Subject completers can be nouns, pronouns, and adjectives. Because the intransitive linking verb links or joins the subject part of the sentence with the verb/predicate part of the sentence, this verb is called an intransitive linking verb. If a pronoun is used, it must be in the subjective case (also known as nominative case) because the subject completer renames the subject. Subject completers are also discussed above in the "Predicate" section under intransitive verbs.

Examples:
The wisdom of the Greek philosopher Socrates becomes more meaningful to me as I continue reading other philosophers' theories.

Becomes is the **intransitive linking verb**; it links *wisdom* with *meaningful*.
Meaningful is the **subject complement** acting as an adjective describing *wisdom*, which, is the **subject**.
Now that's a lot of information. Do you get it?

When asked to name my favorite Greek philosopher, I always respond that it is he, Socrates.
The **intransitive linking verb** would be *is*, which links *it* and *he*.
He is the **subject complement**; that's why the subjective-case pronoun is used.

The sentence could be turned around; then, we see that *he* becomes the subject.

When asked to name my favorite Greek philosopher, I always respond that he is Socrates.

After Socrates, the most intriguing philosopher is Aristotle.
The word *is* would be the **intransitive linking verb**, and it links *philosopher* and *Aristotle*.

Photo © Krivosheev Vitaly, 2011. Used under license from Shutterstock, Inc.

Vivid descriptions excite!

Modifiers

Modifiers describe nouns, pronouns, adjectives, and adverbs. Modifiers can be one word, a phrase, or a clause. A modifier describes or adds information to other parts of the sentence. Adjectives and adverbs are modifiers.

Modifiers add excitement and vitality to writing. Consider the following sentence:
I walked on the beach and saw someone.
A response to that sentence can be, "So what?"

Now, what about this sentence?

Totally confident that I looked really hot because I've been seriously exercising and eating healthy foods, I donned my bright, pink bikini and strolled to the beautiful, nearby beach. I walked on the warm sand just close enough to the ocean to feel refreshed by the ocean spray. Suddenly, I spotted this incredibly alluring person walking directly toward me.

OK, wow! The sentences immediately above with all of those modifiers describes an experience I want to know more about.

Modifiers can be restrictive or nonrestrictive, essential or nonessential, needed or not needed depending on whether the information added is necessary.

My uncle, who lives in Los Angeles, is visiting me.

The commas indicate that the information within them is nonrestrictive; therefore, the reader may conclude that you have just one uncle.

If you were to write, "My uncle who lives in Los Angeles is visiting me," the reader now understands that you have several uncles and are referring to the uncle in Los Angeles; therefore, no commas are used, and the clause is considered restrictive.

Here are two other examples:

My professor Dr. Apple is absent. (Presumably, you have more than one professor; therefore, the proper noun *Dr. Apple* is restrictive, which means that it's essential. Consequently, no commas are needed.)

Dr. Apple, my professor, is absent. (And, here, I'll bet that you have just one professor, Dr. Apple, so you really don't need the words *my professor*; however, the information is useful to the reader. Place commas before and after *my professor* to show that those words are not needed.)

As each of these grammar topics is discussed, notice the punctuation that is used. For example, commas are placed before and after nonrestrictive phrases.

A **clause** is a group of related words containing a subject and predicate (verb). Clauses can function as nouns, adverbs, and adjectives. In this section, we're focusing on clauses functioning as modifiers.

A **phrase** is a group of related words without a subject and predicate. Phrases include noun phrases (gerund and infinitive phrases, which function as subjects, objects, and subjective complements), prepositional phrases and infinitive phrases (which function as adjectives or adverbs), and participial phrases (which function as adjectives). In this section, we're focusing on phrases functioning as modifiers.

As we move through the discussion of modifiers, we will review grammatical structures that act as adjectives and adverbs. Prepositional phrases act as both adjectives and adverbs. Participles and infinitives (which are both verbals) act as adjectives. Read on; there's so much more to this study! I hope you're enjoying it.

Let's look at an **infinitive**. This is a verb form that acts as an adverb and an adjective (a noun, too).

Look! Here's an infinitive used as an adverb:
Marley is ready *to drive*.
The infinitive *to drive* is describing *ready*, which is an adjective. Since adverbs describe adjectives, this infinitive, *to drive*, is acting as an adverb. An infinitive always begins with the word *to* and is followed by a word that is usually a *verb*—for example, **to drive**.

Here is an infinitive as an adjective:
An academic setting encourages the desire to succeed.
The infinitive *to succeed* describes the noun *desire*.
Since the infinitive describes a noun, it is functioning as an adjective.

A **participle** is a verb form used as an **adjective**. It's called a verbal.
I love **burnt** toast.
Burnt is describing the noun *toast*; therefore, *burnt* is functioning as an adjective.

Here is a prepositional phrase as an adverb:
Marley drove **with the window down**.
The phrase *with the window down* is a prepositional phrase telling how Marley drove. Adverbs answer the question *how*. In this sentence, the question is, how did Marley drive? Marley drove **with the window down**. *With the window down* is an adverb prepositional phrase describing *drove*.

Here is a prepositional phrase as an adjective:
Marley is the woman **in the red shorts.**
The prepositional phrase *in the red shorts* is modifying the noun *woman*; therefore, the prepositional phrase is functioning as an adjective.

Now, let's see if the discussion of modifiers—adjectives and adjectives—makes sense to you. At any point in working through these sentences, check the answer page to see if this is clear.

M1 Modifiers—Exercises
(Page 216 Answers)

In the sentences below, identify the words underlined. They are adjectives and adverbs. Check the answers at the end of this guide.

1. Although the pink geraniums are very beautiful, the purple petunias are getting all the attention.

2. Serious gardening requires incredibly strenuous work and is immensely rewarding.

3. I love going out early in the morning to water the delicate flowers.

4. Gardeners are optimists; they demonstrate their belief in the future by planting bulbs for spring bloom.

PP Prepositional Phrases—Exercises
(Page 221-222 Answers)

Place parentheses around the prepositional phrases in the following sentences.

Violence with Guns by Godfrey Sakyi

1. Gun control is one of the most controversial issues in our society.

2. Gun violence in the country has dramatically increased.

3. Is the Second Amendment of the Bill of Rights also a factor in gun violence?

4. Drive-by shootings and gang shootings are committed almost every day.

5. Gangs in the United States are more violent and deadly, hence, increasing gun violence in our society.

6. Can the government stop or reduce the rapid growth of gun violence in the country?

7. The rise of gun violence shouldn't be blamed on violent games, movies, television programs, and song lyrics. The family backgrounds of the violators should be considered.

8. Most crimes in the United States are committed with a gun.

9. What do you think are the causes of gun violence in our society?

10. What can we do to reduce gun violence in our country?

Putting Sentence Parts Together

Grammar is concerned about the rules that govern the standard use of the language. Syntax is how these rules are applied and sentences created. Here, we'll delve into syntax to see how the rules we learned influence the construction of sentences.

In addition to recognizing the parts of a sentence, it is important to understand how to arrange words to make certain of (1) agreement between the subject and the verb, (2) agreement in the number relating to the pronoun and the antecedent, (3) clear pronoun reference, (4) appropriate choice of pronoun case, (5) the correct use of degrees of modifiers, (6) the consistency of verb number and tense, and (7) the correct choice of verb to express mood and (8) voice. Let's spend some time discussing these challenges.

1. Subject/Verb Agreement

The verb and the subject must agree in number; both must be plural or both must be singular. This is challenging when writing in the present tense. Here's why:

Incorrect → The boys plays baseball on Saturdays. (boys/plays)
Correct → The boys play baseball on Saturdays. (boys/play)

In general, when the subject (the doer of the action) has an "s," the verb does not.

Exceptions to rules often bug us. Here's one:
Incorrect → The children plays well together. (children/plays)
Correct → The children play well together. (children/play)

The odd thing is that we learned very early in our language development that an "s" creates the plural. Yes, it does with nouns but not with verbs.

He runs. (Note that the subject, *he*, is singular.)
It runs smoothly. (Note that the subject, *it,* is singular.)

This is called **subject/verb agreement**. Both the **subject** (discussed next) and the **verb** must agree in number. This means that both are singular or both are plural; they have to match.

You want another way to remember this? OK, here goes:

Look at this chart. These are pronouns. (Conjugating verbs, which follows, is also discussed in Chapter 3.)

	Singular	Plural
First person	I	we
Second person	you	you
Third person	he, she, it	they

Let's see what this means.
First person always refers to #1, me, either alone or in a group.
   I am going. (singular)
   We are going (meaning I and others are going.) (plural)

Second person is used to address one other person or to directly address a group.

Do **you**, my child, understand the rules? (you = one)

Do **you**, my children, understand the rules? (you = more than one, a group)

Third person is used to refer to a person or people whom you see over there.

He paints the horses.

She washes the car.

It is a good computer.

They are my best friends.

It's important to understand that the ***third-person, singular, present tense, always takes an s.*** Say this to yourself: third person singular, present tense, always takes an "s." See if you can create a rhythm with those words to help you remember this challenging rule. Chapter 3, "Words (A V CAPPIN)," goes into detail about conjugating verbs in the present tense and highlights the importance of remembering the "S" in third-person singular, present tense.

Another challenging concept in subject/verb agreement is that the phrase **more than one** takes a singular verb, as does the construction **one in six**.

More than one is expected to attend.

One in six has trouble with math in this class.

Correlative conjunctions **either . . .or** and **neither . . .nor** present a different challenge in subject/verb agreement. You need to look at the words being joined.

If the words are plural, use a plural verb.

Either my sisters or my brothers are playing in tonight's competition.

Neither my sisters nor my brothers are playing in tonight's competition.

If the words joined are singular, use a singular verb.

Either my sister or my brother is playing in tonight's competition.

Neither my sister nor my brother is playing in tonight's competition.

2. Agreement of Pronoun and Antecedent

The antecedent is the word that the pronoun must agree with in number, singular or plural. Be consistent in using singular and plural. When using a singular noun, refer to that singular noun with a singular pronoun.

Incorrect → Each student who majored in Hospitality Management hoped they would be selected to intern in a five-star hotel.
Student is singular, yet the word that refers to it is *their*, which is plural. That's inconsistent.
Correct → Each student who majored in Hospitality Management hoped she would be selected to intern in a five-star hotel.
Student is the singular antecedent for the singular pronoun *she*.

When proofreading, make sure that you remain aware of consistent use of singular and plural pronouns.

3. Pronoun Reference to Antecedent

There should be no doubt about the noun to which a pronoun refers. That noun is called the antecedent: the word that precedes the pronoun. In good writing, the reader does not have to search for the antecedent.

Incorrect → Pam and Terri made a party for her husband. *Confusing? Whose husband? To whom does the pronoun refer?*
Correct → Pam and Terri made a party for Terri's husband. (If needed for clarity, repeat the noun.)

4. Cases of Pronouns

"Case" simply reveals how the pronoun functions in the sentence.

I kissed him.
I = subject of the sentence = subjective case
Him = the receiver of the action = objective case

I kissed my brother.
My = possessive case

Here are the pronouns and their cases.

Subjective Case	Objective Case	Possessive Case (never use an apostrophe with possessive pronouns)
I	me	my, mine
you	you	your, yours
he	him	his
she	her	her, hers
it	it	its
we	us	our, ours
they	them	their, theirs

To test to see if the correct pronoun is used, fill in the following blanks with the pronoun that "sounds" right to you. If the pronoun does not sound correct, it's likely that you have selected the wrong one.

Here is an example:
Marty (← **subject pronoun**) studied with **her** (← **object pronoun**) classmates for **their** (← **possessive pronoun**) exams.

Who?_____ (← **subject pronoun**) is kissing whom?_____ (← **object pronoun**) on whose?_____ (← **possessive pronoun**) porch.

See how the following words fit into the blanks above.
I am kissing **him** on **his** porch.

5. Degrees of Adjectives and Adverbs

We use adjectives and adverbs to describe nouns, verbs, adjectives, or adverbs. These words also can indicate the degrees of difference between adjectives and adverbs. This is accomplished by choosing the positive, comparative, or superlative form of the adjective or adverb. Add "er" or "est" to the end of the modifier or "more," "most," "less," or "least" before the modifier to indicate degrees of difference.

If two items are being compared or contrasted, use "er" or "more." When three or more items are being compared, use "est" or "most."

Here are some examples:
The temperature today is **cool.**

The temperature is **cooler** today than yesterday (comparing two days). Tomorrow is supposed to be the **coolest** day of the summer (comparing all the days of the summer).

The dancer's steps are **intricate**.
The teacher's steps are **more intricate** than the student's.
The professional dancer's steps are the **most intricate** of all.

The **comparative degree** is used when comparing two nouns or verbs and use "er" or "more" to show the comparison.

The dog is **friskier** today than yesterday (adjective—comparative degree).
In fact, he ran **faster** than he did yesterday (adverb—comparative degree).

The **superlative degree** is used when comparing three or more nouns or verbs.
Of the three dogs on our block, my dog, Muffin, is the **toughest** (adjective—superlative).
Muffin, my dog, barks the **loudest** of all the dogs in our neighborhood (adverb—superlative).

Muffin is a better student than Maxie (adjective—comparative).
Muffin doesn't win contests because she prances the least gracefully of all the dogs (adverb—superlative).

Let's take a look at degrees of adjectives and adverbs:

Positive	Comparative (two things compared)	Superlative (three or more)
Adverbs		
well	better	best
badly	worse	worst
Adjectives		
good	better	best
small	smaller	smallest
many, much, some	more	most
beautiful	more beautiful	most beautiful
bad (health)	worse	worst

Which **modifiers** should be used with **countable** and **noncountable** nouns? (This is also discussed in "Words" under "Nouns.")

With a noun like **cookies**, use the adjectives fewer or fewest, many or most.

Cookies, as individual items, are **countable**. I have fewer cookies than you. Sandy has the fewest number of cookies of all.

With a noun like **milk**, use the words less or least, more or most. Milk, the liquid, is a **noncountable** noun. (Cartons of milk are countable.) My dog, Rocky, drinks less milk than my cat. Rocky drinks the least amount of milk of all the other pets, including my cat and gerbil.

Note that words like *unique*, *perfect*, *dead*, and *infinite* are *absolute* words and cannot be modified. Therefore, they should not be preceded by *more* or *most*, such as most unique; that's illogical. Something is unique or it's not unique.

Photo courtesy of Andy Feder

This is the *most dismal* station of all on the A line.

6. Consistency in Verb Tense and Number

As you proofread your writing, it is imperative that you confirm that you are consistent in the tense you are using. You need to know **where** you are in the writing, and from that point, you write. Are you in the **present**, writing about the past? Are you in the **past**, writing about the future? Understand where you are and how you're seeing the time frame, and keep the writing logical, clear, and consistent regarding the time you're writing about. Carefully proofread your work to make certain that the tenses are consistent and logical. You don't want the reader to be confused and to spend time wondering about when things occurred; that should be understood without the reader's questioning it.

7. Mood

Three moods are expressed by verbs: indicative, imperative, and subjunctive.

1. The **indicative mood** states a fact or opinion.
   My brother's friends are creeps.
   I'm sure you agree with me.

2. The **imperative mood** expresses a command and generally omits naming the subject. (In Chapter 5, the imperative sentence is discussed.)
   Find decent friends if you want to make something of yourself!

3. **Subjunctive mood** expresses wishes, ideas that are contrary to fact, and uses the word **were**. These sentences generally include the words "if," "wish," and "unless."
   If I **were** you, I would find friends in college not on the street.
   I wish you would value yourself more and choose friends worthy of you.

8. Voice

There are **two voices**: **active** and **passive**. Most writing calls for the active voice.

1. In the **active voice**, the subject performs the action of the verb:
   Finally, my brother found decent friends at the college dances.

2. The **passive voice** may name the actor or doer of the action at the end of the sentence or not at all; in fact, the passive voice generally avoids mentioning who did the action. (See the examples below this paragraph.) The passive voice consists of the verb "to be" and the past participle of the main verb. Only a transitive verb can be used in the passive voice. (*Transitive* is discussed in "Sentence Parts.")

Dances **have been held** weekly at the college. (We don't know who held the dances. That person or group is not mentioned.) Cool people **were invited** to attend by the LGBTQI Club. (The people who did the inviting were named at the end of the sentence.)

Be **consistent** in using **voice** as shifts between passive and active can be confusing to the reader.

S1a, S1b, S1c, S1d Sentence Parts—Exercises (Page 222-224 Answers)

When completed, check the answers at the end of this guide.

S1a Subject/Verb Agreement—Exercises (Page 222-223 Answers)

Circle the correct word.

1. Football players (run/runs) miles a day to keep fit.

2. A football player (exercise/exercises) daily to maintain good muscle tone.

Locate and correct the error in subject/verb agreement.

3. Some teams now hires yoga teachers to train them.

4. Yoga help with balance and concentration.

5. Additionally, yoga assist in keeping muscles healthy through stretching exercises.

6. An effective yoga teacher easily spot players whose posture may hinder healthy alignment of the spine.

7. When seeing incorrect posture, the yoga teacher gently and respectfully place pressure on the part of the body that need to be adjusted.

8. Because individual attention are needed to assure that each player approach yoga postures with care, the teacher should not have too many students.

9. Some teachers hires assistants just to watch the postures so that no one are hurt.

10. When football fans hears that their favorite players does yoga, the fans wants to try yoga, too.

S1b Subject/Verb Agreement—Exercises (Page 223-224 Answers)

Correct the subject/verb agreement errors in the following sentences. As you know, writers are challenged by the third person singular, present tense verb form which invariably requires a final "s." Examples: Marco is a hero. All the students are serious about their work. Not every sentence has an error. There are ten errors.

The Enjoyment of Music by José de la Rosa

1. I always enjoys going to a good music concert, collecting records, and creating music.

2. I loves different styles of music from punk rock, metal, electronic, old school hip hop to more traditional styles like blues, classical, and native music.

3. I could go to an electronic music party and dances all night or sees a punk band and pogo through the whole show.

4. I usually go out with my girl; she is the greatest companion. We always has a good time.

5. She is more into electronic (techno) music than I am.

6. We is thinking about going to two big festivals this year: Coachella in California and Maryland Death Fest in Baltimore.

7. We just bought tickets to see Killing Joke on April 19th at Irving Plaza.

8. Killing Joke are a very prolific English post-punk band that started in the early eighties.

9. I used to be a drummer and sang in a few bands; I was in a total of six bands in a period of seven years.

10. Nowadays, I'm calmer and just has one music project with a friend; we hasn't played any shows yet; we is just in the process of creating tunes.

S1c Pronoun and Antecedent Agreements —Exercises (Page 224 Answers)

1. Simone and Teresa watched (his/her/their) brother play football.

2. They hoped that the players weren't distracted by (his/her/their) presence.

3. When half-time came, the cheerleaders started (his/her/their) routine.

4. One of the cheerleaders dropped (his/their) baton.

5. At that moment, one of the other cheerleaders lost (his/their) balance and screamed as (he/they) fell.

Identify the **subjects** (write S) and **verbs** (write V) in the following sentences in all clauses:

1. Many years ago, Joe Namath was a popular and successful football player.

2. His position was quarterback.

3. His fans were mostly women.

4. He was handsome and charismatic.

5. I really wanted to see him in person.

6. Tickets were so expensive.

7. Actually, the price of tickets for sports events excluded most people from attending the games.

8. However, in cold weather, watching sports at home beats sitting in a freezing stadium.

9. My little brother loves watching games with me.

10. Dad recalls playing football.

11. At that time, all players covered all positions.

12. Watching football at home with my family is really fun.

Choose the correct pronouns in the following sentences. The correct case is determined by the function of the pronoun in the sentence.

1. My friend Teresa and (me/I) watched the guy tumble.

2. (She and I/Her or me) couldn't believe that the baton was flying through the air at the same time.

3. Halftime entertainment, (she/her) said, was never so exciting.

4. We didn't even think about getting hot dogs for (ourself/ourselves).

5. I reminded (she/her) that we'd better get on line for food before halftime events end.

6. Going to sports event with Teresa and (her/she) friends is always fun.

7. Would you like to join (she, he, and I/her, him, and me) next Sunday at the stadium in Coney Island, Brooklyn?

8. I think I love football so much because my dad played for (his/he) high school team.

9. (He/Him), my dad, really enjoyed the game.

10. (His/He) teammates were really strong, and he was so proud of (they/them).

11. His teammates became (his/he/him) lifelong friends.

Choose the correct pronoun in the following sentences.

1. My friend Fran and (I/me) are always dieting.

2. (Her and me/She and I/I and she) like to go out for ice cream every evening.

3. I love socializing with (she/her), but when we're together, the temptation to eat ice cream becomes overwhelming, and (we/us) often give in.

4. We've worked so hard to lose weight, so (she and I/ her and me) feel really disappointed in (ourself/ourselves) when we see the pounds coming back.

5. My doctor weighs (myself/me) every time I go to see (he/him).

6. Fran's doctor weighs (her/she) too.

7. Because (she and I/her and me) eat a variety of healthy foods, that's not the problem.

8. It's about quantity; (me and her/I and she/ she and I) just eat too much.

9. If you have advice for (us/we/ourselves), please, call (me and her/I and she/her and me), and share (you're/your) ideas.

10. (Me and her/ She and me/ her and I/ She and I) really try to behave ourself/ourselves) and (were/we're) going to succeed this time!

M&V1 Mood and Voice—Exercises
(Page 217 Answers)

Correct the next three sentences. (Keep in mind the subjunctive mood.)

1. I would help my brother meet hip kids if I was at his college.

2. If only the kids in high school was to give him a chance, they would know what a sweetheart he really is.

3. If he was straight, bullies would leave him alone.

Identify active or passive voice in the following sentences.

4. A call was received by the Dean of Students about the bullying.

5. My mom called the police.

6. The police notified the school.

7. Those ugly, mean weaklings, victimized my brother.

8. My heart was aching for my little brother.

9. Joining the LGBTQI club helped him feel less frightened and lonely.

10. The LGBTQI adviser and club members offered support, friendship and protection.

Helpful Web Sites

http://depts.dyc.edu/learningcenter/owl/sentences_core_parts.htm

http://grammar.about.com/od/basicsentencegrammar/Understanding_Parts_of_Speech_and_Building_Effective_Sentences.htm

http://grammar.quickanddirtytips.com/subject-verb-agreement.aspx

Notes

Good writing is supposed to evoke sensation in the reader: not the fact that it is raining but the feeling of being rained upon.

—E.L. Doctorow

Notes

Education is the kindling of a flame, not the filling of a vessel.
—Socrates

Photo courtesy of Andy Feder

Wow! I love the challenge of unpredictable terrain!

Chapter 5

Sentence Types

Each conversation we have includes many sentences, yet there are only four kinds of sentences.

1. One kind is used to make a statement: a statement of fact, a statement of opinion. That's called a **declarative sentence**; it declares a point of information.

   A statement of **fact**—The government is offering financial incentives to homeowners to install solar panels to conserve energy.

   A statement of **opinion**—The responsibility for the environment belongs to each one of us.

2. The second kind is an **exclamatory sentence.** Use this style to exclaim or to express **strong emotion**.

   Oh, no! The oil spill has spread thousands of miles and will destroy all the sea creatures in its path.

3. The third kind is an **imperative sentence;** this type of sentence expresses a **command**. (In Chapter 4, the imperative mood is discussed.)

   Everyone must participate in the city's recycling program or risk being fined.

4. The fourth asks a **question**; it's called an **interrogative sentence**.

   Have you considered more effective strategies for preserving our environment?

Read the following sentences; then, identify the **kind of sentence** each is.

1. People on first dates always feel awkward.

2. Be yourself, and you'll make a favorable impression.

3. Come on; go on a date!

4. Don't you want to hang out with kids your own age?

5. Are you intimidated by people you'd like to date?

6. Do you feel vulnerable?

7. Let me assure you; you are as clever and as personable as anyone I know.

8. Here's what you do. Start with something simple.

9. Go out with someone for pizza, and keep it brief.

10. Then, if you have a good time, you'd better give that person another chance!

The benefit of knowing the four sentence types is that if you feel your writing is stiff or becoming monotonous, you can vary the kinds of sentences. You can shift to a question or a command or a strong emotion. Most of our writing consists of declarative sentences. So, knowing these types of sentences and knowing different sentence patterns (as in Chapter 6 "Sentence Patterns") you can add variety to the way you express your ideas. This will certainly contribute to maintaining your reader's interest.

Helpful Web Sites

http://www.worksheetworks.com/english/partsofspeech/sentences/identify-types.html

http://edhelper.com/language/sentences.htm

Notes

The finest language is mostly made up of simple unimposing words.
—George Eliot

Photo courtesy of Andy Feder

Vary the terrain.

Chapter 6

Sentence Patterns

The GPS for Writing

GRAMMAR · PUNCTUATION · SENTENCE STRUCTURE

Transitioning into Sentence Patterns

Having worked through parts of speech, you may be wondering how this will help with your writing. It's when you put words into sentences that all of this knowledge comes in handy. Knowing "Sentence Patterns" will help you to check that all of the word groups are, in fact, sentences and not fragments, fused sentences, or comma splices. Once you have determined that you have constructed the sentences correctly, you may want to see how you can vary the patterns of your sentences, adding more variety and appeal to your writing. This chapter will give you ideas for creating more engaging writing.

The study of **conjunctions** is linked to the study of "Sentence Patterns." The function of conjunctions is to join not only parts of sentences but also sentences. Conjunctions are **joining words**. *Con* means *with*, and *junction* means *joining*.

Let's look at which conjunctions help us to join words that function in similar ways in sentences. (You may want to refer to the chapter "Words (A V CAPPIN)" to review the discussion about conjunctions.)

COORDINATING CONJUNCTIONS

When we want to tell the reader that two or more words, phrases, dependent, and independent clauses are equally important, there are specific conjunctions to join them. But, first, what is meant by **equal** ideas?

You and **I** will go to the movies. **You** and **I** are words representing two people going to the movies; the words **you** and **I** are what the sentence is about; they are the **subjects.** (**Subjects** are discussed in "Sentence Parts.") Therefore, those two words are considered equal to each other. They function in the same way in the sentence; they function as subjects.

Let's look at the following sentence:

The dog barked, **and** the lady jumped.
This sentence is called a compound sentence; this will be discussed later in this chapter.

What is the word **and** joining here?

OK, *and* is joining two independent clauses (two sentences). Neither independent clause appears to be more important than the other; therefore, we can consider them equally important. To test this, try each group of words on either side of the *and* to see if the words can stand alone as a sentence.

The dog barked. OK, that works.
This is called a simple sentence.
The lady jumped. That works, too.

Consequently, we can see that *and* is joining two sentences (independent clauses). So, again, we see that *and* is joining groups of words (clauses) that function in the same way; they are independent clauses (sentences).

Coordinating conjunctions connect similar or equal grammatical structures, as stated above. There are seven coordinating conjunctions.

ABS OF NY

and	or	nor	← Read these words going down each
but	for	yet	column, and you will see that
so			they spell **ABS OF NY**.

(In the chapter "Punctuation," you will learn that (1) every time you use a **coordinating conjunction** to join independent clauses, a comma must precede the conjunction, and, (2) every time a coordinating conjunction joins three or more words, phrases, or clauses, it is preceded by a comma.)

Coordinating conjunctions, like conjunctive adverbs (which are discussed next), form **compound sentences.**

CONJUNCTIVE ADVERBS

These conjunctions, like coordinating conjunctions, join words and word groups. When joining sentences (independent clauses), these words are always preceded by a semicolon (;) and followed by a comma.

A way to remember these words is to look at the first letter of each; then, you will see that they spell **FITCHMINT**. That's a made-up word that may help you to remember conjunctive adverbs. When these words join sentences (independent clauses), they require, yes, a semicolon and a comma.

FITCHMINT—Partial List of Conjunctive Adverbs
furthermore
indeed
therefore
consequently
however
moreover
in fact
nevertheless
then

Let's see how these words are used in sentences. If you find that you are using a lot of commas to join sentences and you want to vary the sentence patterns, try conjunctive adverbs. However, notice that the meaning of the sentence shifts with the conjunctive adverb. Coordinating conjunctions are like an equal sign; both sides of the conjunction express equally important ideas. The conjunctive adverb shows how one idea relates to another. In the following sentence, we see that the barking dog caused the lady to jump.

The dog barked; **then**, the lady jumped.
This sentence is called a compound sentence.

Remembering these words will be very helpful when you write paragraphs and longer compositions.

TRANSITIONAL WORDS

Look at these sentences:

"**In fact**, I do like dogs."
In the preceding sentence, "In fact" is introducing the sentence, not joining two sentences; consequently, "in fact" is not called conjunctive adverbs but transitional words.

If you have allergies, **indeed**, stay away from dogs.

Furthermore, doctors report that the saliva of so-called "safe" dogs may trigger an allergic reaction.

Notice how the placement of **transitional words** affects the flow of the sentence. In this chapter, we continue to develop a common vocabulary for our study of grammar.

Look again at "The dog barked; then, the lady jumped."

Notice that the groups of words on each side of the conjunctive adverb can stand alone; they are independent. Because they can stand alone as sentences, they are called independent clauses.

The dog barked.
The lady jumped.

A *clause* is a group of words that includes a subject and a verb. If this group of words can stand alone, yes, it is an **independent clause**; if not, it is a **dependent clause**. (The difference between the grammatical terms "clause" and "phrase" is that a "phrase*"* is a group of words that does not have both a subject and a verb, and a "clause" has both a subject and a verb.) Again, joining two independent clauses with a coordinating conjunction or a conjunctive adverb creates a compound sentence.

Photo © kropic1, 2011. Used under license from Shutterstock, Inc.

Dependent clauses lean on independent clauses for support.

SUBORDINATING CONJUNCTIONS

Now, if we want to stress one sentence, one independent clause, over another, we use **subordinate conjunctions**. These conjunctions create a clause that cannot stand alone as a sentence. This construction is called a **dependent clause**. Subordinate conjunctions create **complex sentences,** which are discussed below.

Let me show you how to remember several frequently used subordinate conjunctions. Think of the word **WABITS**.

WABITS—Partial List of Subordinating Conjunctions

when
although
because   **WABITS**—These words not only create dependent
if   clauses but also introduce them; dependent clauses
that   are not sentences. Also, the entire dependent clause
since   functions as an adverb because it tells something
                       about the verb.

Let's look at this, especially the part indicating that subordinating clauses function as adverbs.

When the dog barked, the lady jumped.
Look at that! *When the dog barked* tells us *when the lady jumped*. Think of the questions that help us find adverbs: how, when, and where. When did the lady *jump*? She *jumped* when the dog *barked*. Interesting?

I mentioned above that **subordinating conjunctions** create **dependent clauses**. That means they create a group of words that could have been a sentence but is no longer a sentence; the group of words can no longer stand by itself when introduced by a subordinating conjunction.

The dog barked.   ← sentence
Because the dog barked. ← oops, not a sentence; a dependent clause
                          can't stand alone
The lady jumped.   ← sentence
When the lady jumped.   ← oops, not a sentence; a dependent clause
                          can't stand alone

If the above is not clear to you, read each aloud, and I believe you will *feel* that "When the lady jumped" is not a complete idea. More words are needed to complete the idea and make it a sentence. If we just remove the subordinate conjunction, the clause is independent.

Let's play with the following three short, simple sentences. The illustrations will help you to see how the three types of conjunctions discussed above work to offer sentence variety.

Three simple sentences:
Margaret is pregnant.
Margaret is happy.
Margaret has had a healthy pregnancy.

Let's join two of those sentences and make the meaning of both sentences of equal importance. To join two sentences, two independent clauses, let's first use a coordinating conjunction.

Margaret is pregnant, **and** she is happy.

The words on both sides of the **coordinating conjunction** are independent clauses and express ideas of similar importance.

Margaret is pregnant.
She is happy.

Rather than have two sentences, we join them to create a compound sentence, and we'll have sentence variety in our writing.

Let's join two sentences with a conjunctive adverb:
Margaret is pregnant; consequently, she is happy.
Margaret is pregnant; therefore, she is happy.
Both sides of the conjunctive adverb remain independent.

Now, let's join two of these clauses, but let's emphasize one. I want to stress to the reader that Margaret is really happy about being pregnant.

When Margaret is pregnant, she is happy.
Can the first part of this sentence stand by itself?

When Margaret is pregnant ← a piece of a sentence, a dependent
clause, a fragment

Because that part of the sentence can no longer stand alone, it is considered less important than the part that can stand alone, *she is happy*. **Subordinating conjunctions make a clause dependent**; the clause cannot stand by itself as a sentence.

CORRELATIVE CONJUNCTIONS

Like coordinating conjunctions and conjunctive adverbs, correlative conjunctions join equal/like/similar parts of a sentence. **Correlative conjunctions** are particularly interesting because they always come in pairs. Here are some examples.

Neither my brothers **nor** sisters are free to attend the family reunion on that date.

The correlative conjunctions are joining words; here they are joining the subjects of the sentence: brothers and sisters.

Not only my brothers **but also** my sisters can attend the reunion in the summer.
As in the previous sentence, the correlative conjunctions are joining words that function as subjects in the sentence.

The course of study is **not** algebra **but** geometry.
The correlative conjunctions are joining two nouns that are functioning as subject completers.

Correlative Conjunctions
>   neither/nor
>   either/or
>   not/but
>   not only/but also
>   both/and

Sentence Patterns

Now that we've examined how to join clauses to create a variety of sentences, let's look closely at the **four patterns of sentences**.

1. **A simple sentence**—one main idea, one independent clause—may have more than one subject and more than one verb/predicate but all subjects are doing the same actions.

    Subject + Verb.   or   S, S, S + V, V, V.
    Jose smiled.   Jose, Sue, and Mary smiled,
                             laughed, and giggled.
        IC   IC
    Independent Clause   Independent Clause

2. **A compound sentence**—Two or more independent clauses are joined by (1) a comma and a coordinating conjunction or (2) a semicolon, conjunctive adverb, comma.

    Independent clauses are joined by coordinating conjunctions: and, but, so, or, for, nor, yet (Abs of NY).

    S + V, coordinating conjunction (cc) S + V.
    Jose smiled, and Sue laughed.
            IC, cc IC.

Additionally, independent clauses may be joined by conjunctive adverbs that include the words **furthermore**, **indeed**, **however**, and **therefore**.

S + V; conjunctive adverb (ca), S + V.
Jose smiled; however, Sue laughed.
      IC; ca, IC.

The writer may choose a coordinating conjunction or a conjunctive adverb to create sentence variety, to create a different flow between clauses, or to reflect a particular style.

3. **Complex Sentence**—One or more dependent clauses and one independent clause make up a complex sentence. A comma follows the introductory dependent clause. Subordinating conjunctions create dependent clauses. Adding words such as **when**, **although**, **because**, **if**, **that**, **since (WABITS)** to the subject and verb create dependent clauses.

    Subordinating conjunction   SC S + V, S + V.
    When Jose smiled, Sue laughed.
              DC, IC.
    Dependent Clause, Independent Clause

    S + V sc S + V.
    Jose smiled when Sue laughed.
    IC subordinating conjunction DC ← no internal punctuation is
                                  needed

4. **A compound/complex sentence** is more than one independent clause and at least one dependent clause.

    independent clause, coordinating conjunction + independent clause + dependent clause
    Sashi laughed, and Maritza giggled when Shawn sang.
          IC, cc IC DC.

At A Glance—Subordinating and Coordinating Ideas

Creating Simple, Compound, Complex Sentences
Correcting Fragments, Run-on (Fused) Sentences, and Comma Splices

I. **Coordinating Conjunctions**   IC, cc IC. = **Compound Sentence**
     And
     But   *(ABS OF NY)*
     So
     Or
     For
     Nor
     Yet

II. **Conjunctive Adverbs**   IC; ca, IC = **Compound Sentence**
     Furthermore
     Indeed
     Therefore
     Consequently   *(FITCHMINT)*
     However
     Moreover
     In fact
     Nevertheless
     Then

III. **Subordinating Conjunctions**   DC, IC. or IC DC. = **Complex Sentence**
     When
     Although
     Because   *(WABITS)*
     If
     That
     Since

Example of an Independent Clause Simple Sentence
Simple sentence IC = Independent Clause (Subject+Verb): Juan is happy.

Example of a Dependent Clause
DC = Dependent Clause (Subordinating Conjunction+Subject+Verb): When Juan is happy

Examples of Compound Sentences
IC, cc IC. Weekends are fun, and we have time to party.
IC; ca, IC. Weekends are fun; however, we must complete our homework before we party.

Examples of Complex Sentences
DC, IC.   When homework is done, the fun begins!
IC DC.   The fun begins when homework is done.

Examples of Errors
Run-on/Fused Sentences = Juan is happy he finished his work.
Comma Splice = Juan is happy, he finished his work.
Fragment = When Juan is happy.

Here's another example:
dependent clause, independent clause, coordinating conjunction + independent clause
When Tom danced, Sue laughed, and Mary giggled.
DC, IC, cc IC.

Including a variety of sentence patterns will help to bring more creativity, vitality, and appeal to your writing and will help you to avoid common errors in sentence structure.

Errors in Sentence Structure

1. A **fragment** is a group of words that does not have all three elements required in a sentence, **CVS:** complete thought, verb, and subject.
Because I love you. ← missing a complete thought
The school on the corner. ← missing complete thought and verb

2. **Fused or run-on sentences** occur when two sentences, two independent clauses, are joined without the correct punctuation and conjunction.
Examples of errors follow:
My school is on the corner my apartment is on the next block.
Homework can be challenging doing it makes me feel good.

3. **Comma splices** are errors caused by using a comma to join two independent clauses.
Examples of errors follow:
My school is on the corner, my apartment is on the next block.
Homework can be challenging, doing it makes me feel good.

Corrections
Here are a few of the ways to correct these errors:
My school is on the corner. My apartment is on the next block.
My school is on the corner, and my apartment is on the next block.
Homework can be challenging. Doing it makes me feel good.
Homework can be challenging; however, doing it makes me feel good.

Photo © June Marie Sobrito, 2011. Used under license from Shutterstock, Inc.

Doesn't the bridge appear to be joining those two buildings?
This surely looks like compound sentence structure to me!

Chapter 6: *Sentence Patterns*

Identify the pattern by writing simple, compound, complex, or compound/complex sentence.

1. Elyse and Tedra lived next door to each other and were eleven months apart.

2. They were best friends, and they did everything together.

3. They were very adventurous; in fact, they rode their bikes to places they shouldn't have gone.

4. They rode from dawn to dusk.

5. Once when they found a newly constructed chemical plant, they ignored the warning signs and trespassed!

6. This was no place for young kids to play because there were strong odors of chemicals and numerous pools of very dark, gooey liquid.

7. There seemed to be no security guards around, so they wandered down the dirt roads exploring the site.

8. They were utterly amazed when Elyse's mother found them, scolded them for being in this private and dangerous area, and threw their bikes in the back of her truck; then, she drove them home.

9. Rewrite the following as a compound sentence. Use a coordinating conjunction.
   Tedra was a leader. Elyse was a follower.

10. Rewrite the two sentences in #9 using a conjunctive adverb. Choose a work that shows Tedra's behavior caused Elyse's conduct.

11. Rewrite the two sentences given in #9 by joining them with a subordinate conjunction. Emphasize that Elyse followed Tedra.

SP2 Sentence Patterns—Exercises
(Page 227 Answers)

Identify the sentence patterns: simple, compound, complex.

My After-school Life by Ayodele Finch

1. My job every day from 3 PM through 6 PM is being an after-school activity specialist.

2. As a club leader, I run one of the biggest parts of the after-school.

3. The title of the program is Recreational Math.

4. Recreational Math is a gym-based activity that incorporates math, and what I do is help young people become fit and learn new sports all while including math; furthermore, the program also helps the students start learning how to multitask.

5. For example, when the students are playing a soccer game and one of the two teams scores on the other, the team that got scored on (Team A) must come to the blackboard; that team's goalie is excused.

6. The students at the blackboard (Team A) must work as a team to solve the math problem on the blackboard.

7. While this team is at the blackboard (Team A), the team that just scored (Team B) will line up for *free penalty kicks* at their (Team A) goal to score more points.

8. Team A has to work together to solve the math problem quickly to get back in the game because Team B is scoring more points during this time.

9. This game is called *unfair soccer* because I am wrongfully using the penalty kicks rule in order to help the students work as a team, so they don't get scored on.

10. The after-school supervisor created the program because students from this school have a hard time with math and are not in good physical shape for their age.

11. The students are very interested in Recreational Math; they find it to be very challenging, so they feel proud knowing that they didn't just beat their opponent with their physical skills but with their mental skills as well.

12. Having the chance to do Recreational Math with the students shows me that students tend to learn a little better when they are in a friendly competition with their classmates because striving to be number one always makes them try harder, and that's just fantastic.

13. The whole purpose of an after-school program is to assist the morning subject teachers in helping the students understand everything that they are currently learning.

14. For this to happen, both morning and after-school staff need to communicate effectively to get the best out of the students.

SP3 Sentence Patterns—Exercises
(Page 228 Answers)

Identify the pattern of the sentences below: simple, compound, complex, compound/complex.

Drawing by Elsa Hadad

1. I never realized before that I have drawing talent.

2. My father provided me with a second-hand drawing magazine that he got from his friend.

3. I have imitated many drawings since I was four.

4. My father had encouraged me to draw.

5. Drawing for me is recreational activity; I spend a lot of time practicing drawing.

6. I will never stop learning how to draw better.

7. Hand sketching, Auto Cad, and Revit are part of the drawing techniques that I have learned.

8. I remember when my father passed away, and my mom told me that my father wanted me to become an architect.

9. We all know that architects transfer their ideas to drawing plans.

10. My father encouraged me to draw when I was four, and I never stopped.

11. I am happy that I can make his wish come true.

12. I do believe that he smiles from above knowing that I have been drawing all my life.

SE1 Sentence Errors—Exercises (Page 225 Answers)

In the following sentences, identify fragments, run-on sentences, and comma splices by writing the letters F, RO, and CS.

1. Television takes up so much of my time the shows are boring this year.

2. Except the reality shows.

3. My brothers watch prison reality shows, they scare me.

4. Is the purpose of those shows to frighten us they do.

5. Scared straight from prison.

When proofreading your work, check to see if you have variety in sentence patterns and your writing is free from the three errors in sentence structure.

Identify and correct the errors in sentence structure. You will find fragments, run ons (fused sentences), and comma splices. Not all sentences have errors.

The Story in Progress by Daniel Huerta

1. I was going to join the Army, my ankle operation delayed my plans.

2. Because I have had an ankle problem since childhood. My plans for my future had to be delayed.

3. In order to join the Army. I would have to lose a massive amount of weight.

4. I would like to be the leader of my squad in the Army, I have good leadership skills.

5. Wanting to be in the battlefield is my greatest goal.

6. Serving this country can make many proud of me my parents and friends will be especially happy for me.

7. Once I got the hang of things in the Army. I was thinking of joining the Marines

8. Being in the Army is a life-changing experience it will make me a more independent man

9. For me, being in the military is going to be of great importance I will become more disciplined.

10. Serving in the military will be an adventure. To be told to my family for generations.

Helpful Web Sites

Verb Phrase
http://en.wikipedia.org/wiki/Verb_phrase

Subordinate adverb clauses
http://www.rockpicklepublishing.com/essays/
complexsentencessubordinateclausesadverbclauses.html

Run-on sentences
http://grammar.quickanddirtytips.com/run-on-sentences.aspx

Fragments
http://grammar.quickanddirtytips.com/sentence-fragments-grammar.aspx

Comma Splices
http://grammar.quickanddirtytips.com/comma-splice.aspx

English Sentence Patterns
www.manythings.org/e/patterns.html

Notes

What is the shortest word in the English language that contains the letters: abcdef? Answer: feedback. Don't forget that feedback is one of the essential elements of good communication.

—Author Unknown

Photo courtesy of Andy Feder

Punctuation marks, like signposts, indicate directions.

Chapter 7

The GPS for Writing

GPS **P** is

★ Active route
Passive route 19:34 42mph

GRAMMAR • PUNCTUATION • SENTENCE STRUCTURE

Punctuation

As we continue with *The GPS for Writing*, our navigation system for effective writing, let's consider punctuation marks as signposts; they tell the reader and writer to pause, to stop, to move logically and smoothly through ideas. Punctuation marks complement and underscore emotion and assist in establishing rhythm and tone. Read the explanations of punctuation marks to see how they actually work.

If you are using this information in an academic community, check with each professor to see which style guide is being followed as rules may be different (more or fewer) from those indicated below. Some of the style guides include those published by the Modern Language Association (MLA), the American Psychological Association (APA), and the Chicago Manual of Style (CMS).

What you will find in all writing communities is the requirement to **be consistent** in your use of punctuation marks.

Apostrophe (')

An apostrophe is used to show omission of letters and numbers, to shorten words to create contractions, and to show possession. Additionally, some style guides state that the apostrophe should be used to form the plural of capital and lower case letters (a's and A's) to avoid confusion. Without the apostrophe, the plural of "a" or "A" looks like "as" or "As" which, certainly, would confuse the reader.

Contractions

A contraction is the combination of two words into one. It eliminates or omits one or more letters. The apostrophe is inserted in the space of the eliminated letters or numbers.

> Do not = Don't
> He will = He'll
> I grew up in the '90s. (Omitted "19" from the decade 1990s.)

An apostrophe is also used when a single word is shortened. Place the apostrophe where the letters have been omitted.

> Brooklyn = B'klyn

There is no hard and fast rule to create contractions or to shorten words. Using a dictionary and consulting style guides will provide the most common contractions and shortenings as well as abbreviations of words.

CO Contractions—Exercises
(Page 210 Answers)

The apostrophe is used in the following sentences to create contractions. They are places where letters are missing. Write the words that would appear if there were no apostrophes.

Example:
I'm eager to read about Krystal.
I'm = I am

Krystal by Elias Salaam

1. Krystal's my best friend; we met back in high school.

2. I've known her for only one year and a few months, but as soon as we met for the first time, we got close pretty fast.

3. She's really trustworthy and friendly.

4. She might have a few flaws here and there, but no one is perfect, so I'm glad I met her.

5. Krystal has always been there for me when I've needed her.

6. I'd talk to her about anything, and she won't ever judge me, even if it's bad.

7. She gives me advice about how to fix things.

8. She's in college right now, so I don't see her that much, but we always keep in touch.

9. She has a great personality and a great sense of humor.

10. We're never bored talking to each other.

11. One of the reasons we got so close is because we both like playing games; Call of Duty is our favorite.

12. She's awesome!

Plurals

As mentioned above, if there is a possibility of confusion, use the apostrophe to form plurals of letters.

Sammie earned all A's in her courses. (The apostrophe avoids confusion with the word As. The same applies to the plural of the letter I, I's; use an apostrophe to avoid confusion with the word Is.)

Italics will often be effective in pluralizing letters; therefore, the apostrophe will not be used.
We have the same initials; consequently, to avoid confusing the two *JFs*, I'll add the first initial of my middle name, JTF.

Since there is no confusion in writing the plural of numbers, do not use an apostrophe to pluralize numbers.

My favorite music is from the 1960s, Rock 'n' Roll. (Note, the apostrophes before and after **n** indicate missing letters for the word **and**.)

Possession

The apostrophe is always placed on the owner or owners; the things owned *never* require an apostrophe. In order to determine placement of the apostrophe, the following strategy will help:
First, determine the owner(s) and what is owned.
Next, **convert the sentence** to make the relationship clear.

Example: The boys' books are on the shelf.
When converted, the sentence becomes, "The books owned by the boys are on the shelf."

Example: The children's books are on the floor.
When converted, this sentence becomes, "The books owned by the children are on the floor."

Rule for placement:
If the owner ends with an "s," place the apostrophe after the "s"; e.g., write the boys' books.
If the owner ends with a letter other than "s," place the **apostrophe and "s"** at the end of the word; e.g., write the children's books.

To confirm placement of the apostrophe, **reorder the words** in the sentence and add **of**.
Let's look at the following sentence.
  The boys books are on the table. Is an apostrophe need in this sentence?

  Are we referring to one boy or many boys?
  Let's say we want to refer to one boy. Now, reorder the words: the books **of** one boy.
  Since the word boy does not end in "s," add an apostrophe and an "s" to create the possessive.

The boy's books are on the table.

When referring to many boys books, first, reorder the words: the books **of** many boys.
Since the word boys ends in "s," we add the apostrophe after the "s'" to make boys possessive.

The boys' books are on the table.

Remember that the possessive apostrophe is placed on the owner not the thing owned.

P1 Punctuation Apostrophe—Exercises (Page 217-218 Answers)

Choose the word with the correct apostrophe. If no apostrophe is needed, indicate that.

1. (It's/Its/Its') always the responsibility of the speaker to make sure that her message is understood.

2. Sometimes, even if there's just one speaker, the (speakers/speaker's/speakers') intention is confusing to the listener.

3. Most (teacher's/teachers/teachers') lessons are planned so that all of the students can grasp the concept.

4. It is the (student's/students/students') responsibility to make certain that they're clear about the concepts taught.

5. (Professor's/Professors'/Professors) are eager to help all of their (students, student's, students') grasp the concepts taught.

6. After many (day/day's/days') preparation, the new teacher finally created a clear, fun, and effective lesson.

7. The (students/student's/students') enjoyment of the lesson and their learning were evident when they were discussing the subject at the end of class.

8. Do you think that (professors/professor's/professors') salaries should depend on the success of their students?

9. I (would of/would've) become a teacher if I felt I could express myself clearly.

10. Speech classes (shouldnt'/should'nt/shouldn't) be eliminated from the curriculum because everyone needs to communicate clearly no matter what profession (he's/his/hes') or (shes/shes'/she's) studying.

Brackets [ ]

When adding information to a quotation, modifying someone else's words, or clarifying within a quotation, use (square) brackets around the words added.

Example
The athletic director announced, "The teams [girls in first-string basketball] are to refrain from drinking alcohol, specifically during the basketball season."

Capitalization (CAPITALIZATION)

When should a word be capitalized? Capitalization is the use of upper-case letters (as opposed to lower-case letters). When the first letter of a word is capitalized, that's called the initial capital; capitalization refers to using an initial capital for a word. There are three simple rules for when to use capital letters: (1) for words that start a **new sentence**, (2) for **proper nouns**, and (3) for words in a **title**.

1. Use a capital letter at the **beginning of a sentence**, in other words, after a period, exclamation mark, or question mark. Each new sentence starts with a word that has an initial capital letter. When a colon introduces an independent clause, the first word after the colon is often capitalized, but some publications use a lower case letter.

2. Use a capital letter when a word is a **proper noun**, that is, the name of something. That name could be the name of a person, for example, Lee Davis. It could also be the name of a company, such as Microsoft or Toyota or the name of a product like Dove soap or Rice Krispies. When part of a name, a person's title is capitalized, as in Senator Smith. The word *senator* is capitalized in the preceding sentence because it's part of the senator's name. If we are just talking about senators in general, the word "senator" is not capitalized because it is not a part of a name.

3. Use capital letters for **titles** of books, plays, movies, or other works of literature. Look at the title of the report "The Toxicology

Report on the Hispanics in Queens" by the Bellevue Research Lab.

The nouns, *toxicology, report, research,* and *laboratory* are all capitalized in the title because they constitute the name of the report. "Bellevue Research Lab" is capitalized because it's the name of the laboratory. The words *Hispanics, Queens,* and *Bellevue* are always capitalized because they are proper nouns.

Titles of books, *Harry Potter and the Chamber of Secrets,* and movies, *Star Wars,* are also written with initial capital letters because they are the names of those works. Certain words in titles are not capitalized unless they are the first or last word of the title. In the examples above, the words *on, the, in, and* are not capitalized.

A Note about Capitalization and Words in Titles	
Words that should be capitalized in titles: • The first word of the title • The last word of the title • Any word of four letters or more • All words in titles of three words or fewer	Words that should NOT be capitalized in titles: • Articles • Coordinating conjunctions • Prepositions with fewer than four letters • "To" when part of a verb phrase that is not at the beginning of the title

Another instance of capital letters being used is in abbreviations such as IBM for International Business Machines (the name of a company, a proper noun) or mnemonics such as A V CAPPIN. In these cases, the words are entirely made up of capital letters, also known as block capitals. (A mnemonic is a device that is used to help a person remember something; in the case of A V CAPPIN, the letters help you remember the parts of speech.)

Most of this may already be familiar to you. However, writers often run into problems with capitalization when they capitalize words that are not proper nouns but that they want to emphasize. Here's an example: "The Elephant ran away from the Circus." This capitalization is

wrong! *Elephant* and *Circus* should **not** have an initial capital letter because neither is a proper noun. However, if the sentence were, "The elephant ran away from the Big Apple Circus," the name of the circus would be capitalized, although, again, the noun *elephant* would not be.

Colon (:)

The colon follows an independent clause, a sentence: a group of words with a subject, verb, and a complete thought. ← This sentence uses a **colon to introduce a phrase.**

However, the writer may use a colon as follows: "Hey, wait! Don't stop reading here: read the next few words before you fully stop." A **colon can introduce an independent clause.** Take notice of the colon in the preceding sentence?

When a colon introduces a sentence, either a capital letter or a lower-case letter may be used. Just **be consistent** in your choice.

If an independent clause follows the colon, it's often modifying what precedes the colon.

Example:
An independent clause precedes a colon: An independent clause may also follow a colon and often modifies the first independent clause. ← You may need to reread this sentence as it is an example of the rule it's stating.

A colon differs from a semicolon because it may be followed by a phrase; a semicolon must be followed by an independent clause. A colon is more formal than a semicolon.

A colon may also be used
1. after a formal salutation in a letter
   Dear President:
2. when writing the time
   It's 12:05. We're late for lunch!
3. before a quotation (generally a formal quotation rather than a conversation, where a comma is preferred)
   Shakespeare's Hamlet said: "To be, or not to be, that is the question."

Comma (,)

OK! Now, let's demystify, simplify, clarify; let's, finally, figure out the correct use of the comma. I assure you that if you understand the next few rules, you will have mastered the correct use of the comma. Refer to the chart on page 86, "At A Glance--Subordinating and Coordinating Ideas" to review explanations of Abs of NY, FITCHMINT, and sentence patterns.

The most important concept to remember is that punctuation marks are intended to ease communication; without them, miscommunication could occur. Therefore, their placement should be logical; they should not be intrusive but rather help the words flow. Be consistent in how punctuation marks are used. Use them sparingly; when in doubt, leave them out!

1. In **compound sentences**, always place a comma before a **coordinating conjunction** (ABS OF NY) and after a **conjunctive adverb** (FITCHMINT) when they join independent clauses.

   My mother enjoys wearing a bikini, and her friends remark about how slender she is. IC, cc IC.

   The ocean waves and riptides have been strong this summer; therefore, Mom hasn't worn her bikini! IC; CA, IC.

2. Place a comma after an **introductory** word, phrase, or clause and before tags at the end of sentences. As we want to separate introductory elements from the main clause of the sentence, we also want to separate tags. Tags are words added at the end of a sentence and not essential to the main idea of the sentence.

   Examples:
   In fact, if you exercised daily, you, too, would be in good shape like my mom.

   Every morning at 7, Mom is on the treadmill reading *The New York Times*.

   When the waves are rough, she knows better than to wear her bikini.

   Robert wants to go to the beach with us, right?

3. Place a comma around **nonessential** and **interruptive** elements.

We do, of course, have an effective cooler to make sure the food doesn't spoil.

Fran, one of my friends from childhood, enjoys swimming with my mom. (If I were to write, "My friend from childhood Fran likes to swim with my mom." I would not place commas around "Fran" because I have many friends from childhood, so Fran's name is essential in the second sentence.)

My mom does, in fact, enjoy a nutritious diet and is mindful of her caloric intake.

4. Place a comma before, after or around the name of a **person spoken to** depending where in the sentence the name appears.

Tem, are you going to swim in the ocean today?

Are you, Tem, going to swim in the ocean today?

5. Place a comma after each item in a **series** of words, phrases, and clauses. (Alert! Some journals now have eliminated the final comma before the conjunction.)

Jellyfish, mussels, and clams were left on the shore after the storm.

The children played with the beach ball, with the badminton set, and with the volleyball.

6. Placement of commas that you may already know and certainly have been using are in the examples below:
   a. before quotations—I asked Mom, " How are you feeling?"
   b. addresses—I live at 18 Hudson Street, Brooklyn, New York.
   c. numbers—I have 1,000 books in my library.
   d. dates—My birthday is May 15, 1975.
   e. between day, month, and year—I'll see you Tuesday, December 15, 2015.
   f. between name and title—Barack Obama, President

OK—that's the deal. Work on those six uses of commas.

Certainly, to correctly use rule number one, you must understand sentence parts and patterns, i.e., independent clauses and compound sentences. Although *The GPS for Writing* allows you to begin at any point, the content starts with the word, discusses functions of words, puts words into sentences, and explores ways to join sentences. There is a logical progression; one chapter builds on the information from the preceding chapter.

The philosophy that guides this approach is the belief that to write well the writer needs to have an understanding of the basics of grammar and the subsequent steps of composing or writing sentences. Then, of course, come the punctuation marks, the road signs that tell the reader to read on, to slow down, to stop, or to emphasize one idea over another.

Photo courtesy of Jane Tainow Feder

The comma keeps ideas moving.

C1 Comma—Exercises
(Page 208 Answers)

There are ten comma errors in the sentences below. Add or remove commas following the rules in this chapter.

Competitive Sports by Fred Worell

1. I like watching, sports.

2. Mostly I like watching basketball, and football.

3. My favorite basketball team is, Oklahoma City Thunder.

4. My favorite football team is, the New York Giants.

5. I also like playing sports, with my friends.

6. My favorite sports to play are basketball football and handball.

7. I like watching sports because they are competitive.

8. I like playing because I like competing against my friends and it also keeps me in shape.

9. Also it's a lot of fun to beat my friends.

10. Playing sports teaches me how to work with others.

C2 Comma Placement—Exercises
(Page 208-209 Answers)

There are fourteen comma errors in the sentences below. Add or delete commas following the rules in this chapter.

Leaving Taiwan for the USA by Peter (Chein-chang) Li

1. I left my parents and Taiwan, and moved to the United States twenty-eight years ago.

2. I brought my new wife to the United States, and without any relatives or friends around us we started a new adventure.

3. I departed my job as a cargo ship sailor and she left her nursing job.

4. By learning about the American experience from television I had promised her that the USA was full of opportunities to learn English, look for jobs, and live in a big house.

5. We hoped that we would survive and save money in the bank. Then we would be able to buy a used car and drive it to supermarkets, the laundry, and to furniture stores.

6. Eventually we will buy our house in the suburbs and move to our sweet home with our car.

7. We will have children and they will play baseball on our green grass in our backyard.

8. We want to make our dreams come true in this journey in spite of the opposite opinions from families.

9. Now, many years have passed by and we have fulfilled our goals.

10. We have experienced that life in America is like a variety of flavors; sometimes it is sour like hot-and-sour soup, sweet like ice cream, bitter like bitter herbs, and hot like Mexican hot chili.

11. We understand the laws, and respond to Court Summons to pay parking tickets.

12. I often parked the car where it was convenient for me; consequently I learned the lesson to obey parking signs by sitting in the courts and paying the fines.

13. We are grateful to the volunteers, for teaching us English because we were so eager to adapt to this new life.

14. Our English teachers were from the local senior citizen organizations, and the classrooms were the local libraries and supermarkets. That was our first schooling experience, in the USA.

Dashes (Em Dash—) (En Dash–)

Oops—oh, no—I did it again! I changed my mind. Do you want to go—to the movies, I mean—with us tonight? See, the em dash is made with two hyphens. Type them together and the typing program will create one line —. The em dash is used to mark a break in thought or to signify that something very important is about to happen. An mm dash, often made with two hyphens--becoming the length of the letter "m" thus its name--can be used in pairs or on its own. It should not be used too often, as writing should advance logically and not have too many breaks or interruptions of thought. There are no spaces before or after the dash.

An en dash is about the length of the letter "n." Consider substituting the word "to" for the en dash. For example, I went to school September -January. Read chapters 4-8 for homework. En dashes also are used to join two words that are acting as one to describe a noun: She is a self-made millionaire. As you see, en dashes act like hyphens, too. (See explanation of hyphens below.)

Ellipsis Mark (. . .)

This punctuation is composed of three dots (periods) with one space in between each dot and indicates that some material is missing or, when at the end of a sentence, may indicate a longing or wistful thought. Text messaging uses ellipses (plural) to indicate that the message continues on or, again, that words are deliberately omitted.

Although successful, he didn't flaunt his achievements.
Although he was . . . successful is a clause; *he was* is understood; it's elliptical. The group of words beginning with **although** is a dependent clause. Within the clause, there may be ellipsis where the subject and verb are implied.

Photo courtesy of Andy Feder

Stop! Read! Think! Go!

Exclamation Mark (!)

This mark (also known as an exclamation point) is used to emphasize the idea expressed in the sentence. Strong emotion, cautions, and commands are followed by exclamation marks.

An exclamation mark follows an exclamatory sentence. Use these marks sparingly, or they will lose their impact on the reader.

Hyphen (-)

When two words function as one, generally as adjectives followed by a noun, join them with a hyphen. The en dash also functions in this way. This is discussed above in Dashes.

Example:
The well-built barn withstood the devastating windstorm.

Example:
Pro-choice advocates were guest lecturers in the Women's Studies class.

Use a hyphen after prefixes: all-, self- (except for selfless and selfish), and ex- (meaning former). There are other prefixes that work well with a hyphen; because the rule is not strict and the use of the hyphen is changing, check the most recent copy of the style guide you prefer to follow, and go with that.

Examples:
ex-husband
self-conscious
all-inclusive

Italics (*Italics*)

Italic type is the type used in this sentence. It is a slanting version of the font used, and that slant is always to the right. The original italic type was used in 1501 in Italy—the genesis of the word *italic*.

When is italic type used? In most scholarly writing, italics are used for the name of works of fiction and nonfiction. For example, the movie *Star Wars* and the title of the book *Ease Your Way: Basics for Writers* are italicized, that is, written in italic font, because they are titles of the works.

Here is the rule: If the writing is long, that is, a full-length work, the title is italicized; if the work is short, the title is put in quotation marks. So, the name of the full-length newspaper is *The New York Times* and that name is italicized, but individual articles (short works) within the newspaper are put in quotation marks: "Tempest in a Tea Party." Also, the title of Lady Gaga's music album (a long work) is *Born This Way*, and that title is italicized. The individual song (a short work) is put in quotation marks: "Born This Way." It's a type of code that has been developed to let people know whether they are dealing with a major work or something short. Here's a list of the types of publications that have italicized titles.

Titles Written in *Italics*		
Titles of Full-Length Novels Titles of Full-Length Films Titles of Full-Length Plays Titles of Book-Length Poems Titles of MP3s, CDs, Cassettes, or Albums Titles of Television Series	Titles of Newspapers Titles of Magazines Titles of Periodicals Titles of Complete Books Titles of Encyclopedias Titles of Pamphlets	Visual Artworks Names of Paintings Names of Sculptures Names of Drawings Names of Mixed Media Works
Note that the names of traditional religious works (Bible, Koran, Torah) are capitalized but never italicized or underlined.		

Italics are also used for non-English words in an English text: The indigenous people of South America call the earth *Pachamama*. One of the noteworthy features of the English language is how easily it adopts foreign words. Once a foreign word is adopted, it is no longer italicized, so words like **laissez-faire**, **et al**., and **ad hoc**, while foreign in origin, are not written in italics.

Finally, italics are used to set certain words apart from others. Quotation marks and bold type can serve the same purpose.

Parentheses ( )

When a writer wishes to give additional information not needed to get the point across (for example dates or a brief definition of a word), that material is generally enclosed in parentheses. (The spelling of *parenthesis* is *es* when plural and *is* when singular.)

If the words within the parentheses are a sentence, the punctuation is within the parentheses, as above.

If the parenthetical expression is within the sentence, the punctuation comes after the parentheses, as in the sentence below.

Although my morning class starts at 6 (when most students are sleeping), my students arrive promptly.

Photo courtesy of Andy Feder

Signs and signals help us stay on the right road.

Period (.)

The period is a final punctuation mark after a declarative sentence, a sentence that makes a statement.

Question Mark (?)

A question mark ends an interrogative sentence, a sentence that asks a question. This is a final punctuation mark just like the period and the exclamation mark. When a question expects no answer (merely rhetorical), do not use the question mark.
Won't you please join us on Friday for dinner.

Quotation Marks (" ")

Quotation marks indicate the exact words of someone other than the writer. The period, the comma, and the exclamation mark precede the quotation marks. The question mark comes after the quotation marks only when the quotation is within a sentence that asks a question.

Example:
Did your teacher say, "Do your homework tonight"?
You see that the quotation is not a question; this is an interrogative sentence. Therefore, the quotation marks precedes the question mark. If a question mark, dash, or exclamation mark applies only to the full sentence, place the mark outside the quotation marks, as in the example above.

Occasionally, there is a need for **single quotation marks**. They are used to indicate a quotation within a quotation (also known as an internal quotation).

Example:
Did you hear Manya say, "The professor said, 'You must complete the work by Monday'"?

Notice that at the end of the quotation, three punctuation marks are indicated: a single for the internal quotation, a double for the fuller quotation, and the question mark. Because the entire sentence is a question, the question mark follows the quotation marks.

Semicolon (;)

Placement of the semicolon is guided by three rules.

1. Place a semicolon between two independent clauses (sentences) not joined by a coordinating conjunction (ABS OF NY).

   Tickets to sports events are monstrously expensive; most of my friends cannot afford to attend games.

2. Place a semicolon before a conjunctive adverb when it joins two independent clauses. (A comma is placed after the conjunctive adverb, FITCHMINT.)

   Tickets to sports events are monstrously expensive; therefore, most of my friends cannot afford to attend games.

3. Place a semicolon between items in a series for clarity.

   The friends who would love to go to sports events are Tess, my best friend; Charlie, my sister's girlfriend; Andy, my childhood friend; and Sam, my college study partner.

Slash (/)

A forward slash (/) is a punctuation mark. A backslash (\ ) is a typographical mark. So, let's look at the forward slash and see what it tells us about how words are functioning in a sentence.

The forward slash may be used to replace the hyphen or dash to indicate a clear joining or relationship between two words; examples are **and/or**, **he/she**. (The latter is discouraged by many writers because it's clumsy).

The slash is an efficient and economical mark to **separate options** (and/or), to indicate the **end of a line of poetry**, and to mark parts of an **electronic address**.

Underlining (____)

Before the widespread use of word processors, underlining (also called underscoring) and italics were used in the same way. Writers would choose one—italics or underlining—and use it throughout their papers. The use of word processors has made underlining obsolete. Most writers use italic type as the favored method of indicating full-length titles and foreign words; underlining should be avoided. If electronic environments do not allow the use of italics, writers should put one line before and one line after the titles that would be italicized: _My Cousin Vinnie_.

P2 Punctuation—Exercises
(Page 218 Answers)

Review the sentences below. Are the correct punctuation marks appropriately placed in the sentences? If not, write in the correct punctuation where it belongs. If correct, write "C" for correct.

1. The ocean reflects the weather, and the waves are telling us that a storm is brewing.

2. Many people find it impossible to be friends—or even friendly—with their expartners.

3. The new farmers were very pleased to find a well built barn on the property that they had just purchased.

4. The massive antique clock stood proudly in the hallway.

5. The principal said, Please, raise your hand.

6. We recited, "I pledge allegiance to the flag . . ." at the beginning of each class session.

7. My sister teaches at New York City College of Technology (part of CUNY).

8. As soon as the sun rises the fog will begin to disappear.

9. Women's rights have been eroded in recent years; this suggests that civil rights for all are being threatened.

10. The current state of our country is abysmal. We face challenges in so many areas: economic stability, relationships with other countries, and constructive partnerships within our own government.

P3 Punctuation—Exercises
(Page 219-220 Answers)

Insert the omitted punctuation marks throughout these sentences. Not every sentence needs a punctuation mark. Look for a total of fifteen marks.

Soccer, Once My Favorite Sport by Jovian Rutherford

1. My favorite sport of all time is soccer.

2. When I was a child I wanted to be a soccer player.

3. Now that I am grown I dont want to be a soccer player anymore.

4. People used to say "You should be a basketball player. You're too tall to play soccer."

5. I never listened much to what people had to say because soccer was my passion.

6. When I was younger I used to play soccer in the park all the time.

7. My dad used to bring me to Marine Park in Brooklyn N.Y. every day after school to practice soccer.

8. Even though I dont watch soccer anymore on television I like to keep up with whats going on in the leagues today.

9. I am from a Caribbean background where soccer is the most popular sport.

10. Although all my relatives were once soccer players no one make it professionally.

11. All my relatives were once soccer players even though no one made it professionally.

12. After moving to the United States I found inspiration in watching basketball.

13. The similarities between soccer and basketball are aggressive players and constant running.

14. The difference between basketball and soccer is in basketball you use your hands and in soccer it is strictly about using your feet.

15. On a soccer field, there are eleven players on the field for each team including a goalkeeper also referred to as a goalie.

16. In basketball only five players are allowed on the basketball court for each team.

17. In soccer, scoring a goal is one point; in basketball, scoring a basket is two or three points.

18. I think I will change my favorite sport from soccer to basketball because soccer is less popular in America.

19. What is your favorite sport

20. Is soccer your favorite sport, too?

Helpful Web Sites

http://www.superteacherworksheets.com/punctuation.html

http://www.savethecomma.com/game/

http://www.oswego.org/ocsd-web/quiz/mquiz.asp?filename=
kderittepun

http://grammar.quickanddirtytips.com/punctuating-questions.aspx

Notes

Freedom is not worth having if it does not include the freedom to make mistakes.

—Mahatma Gandhi

Let's see how words relate to one another.

Chapter 8

The GPS for Writing

GPS

Active route
Passive route 09:16 14mph

GRAMMAR · PUNCTUATION · SENTENCE STRUCTURE

Diagramming Sentences

Sentences in Diagrams

If you are a visual learner, diagramming sentences may be very helpful, for it offers a different view of a sentence, one that shows how words interact with one another.

Let's start with what's referred to as the base line. This straight horizontal line is a base line.

First, work with the sentence:
Summer vacationers happily eat mangoes.

The **verb/predicate** tells the time (tense) and describes what the subject is doing.

Divide the base line in half with a vertical line cutting through the base line. To the right of the line, write the verb.

eat

The **subject** is what the verb is talking about. Write the subject to the left of the vertical line. If the subject begins the sentence, carry the capital letter into the diagram.

vacationers | eat

Modifiers (describers) add to the meaning of nouns and verbs. Write the modifier under the word it modifies.

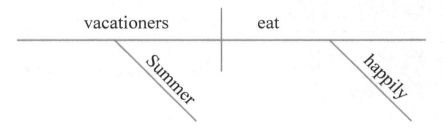

Objects are defined in the section "Sentence Parts." Take the verb and ask *what* or *whom*? If there is an answer, draw a vertical line up to the baseline after the verb. Place this word to the right of that vertical line. This word is the **direct object**, the receiver of action from the (transitive) verb.

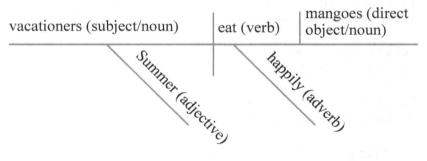

Here's another example of a sentence with modifiers and a direct object: *New York's firefighters courageously stormed the burning Twin Towers.*

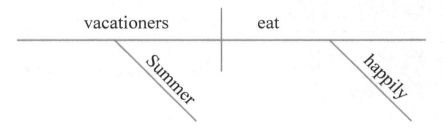

Look at the next example; consider how the words are functioning in the sentence. See whether you can figure out the word order from the diagram. The diagram above includes a verb that sends action to a recipient (a transitive verb followed by a direct object). Notice that the line after the verb is vertical. This next diagram has a verb that does not send action (an intransitive verb). This verb links the subject with the subjective complement (an adjective, noun, or pronoun) found in the predicate part of the sentence. Observe the position and length of the line after the verb. This is an intransitive verb followed by a subject completer (subjective complement).

Firefighters	are	heroic

Here's a review of diagramming and the placement of words based on how they function in the sentence. You will also see how words interact with one another. The first is an example of a sentence with a transitive (action) verb and a direct object.

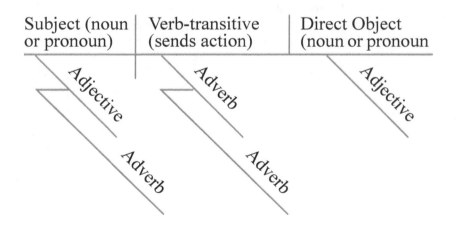

Subject (noun or pronoun)	Verb-transitive (sends action)	Direct Object (noun or pronoun
Adjective / Adverb	Adverb	Adjective

Amazingly skilled, Derek Jeter very masterfully fielded the speeding ball.

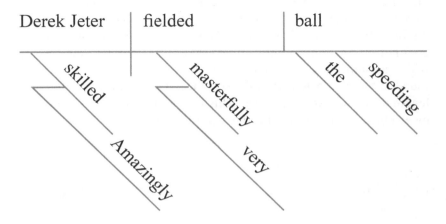

Below is an illustration of a sentence with an intransitive verb (one that does not produce action), subject completer, and a prepositional phrase. Since the prepositional phrase hangs from the subject completer, it is modifying the subject completer/noun; thus, it is an adjective prepositional phrase.

Tom Hanks is an actor of astonishing talent.

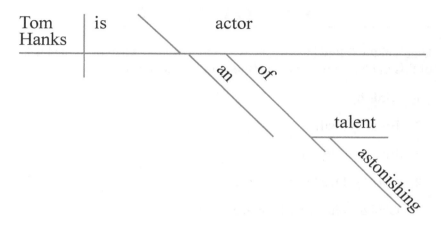

Now you try. Here are steps to help you create sentence diagrams.

How to Diagram a Sentence

1. Start by locating the word that signifies time, the verb.

2. Take the verb and ask *who* or *what*: *who* or *what* did the action?

3. Next, see if the verb is acting upon another word by adding *whom* or *what* to the verb; that will give you the direct object. If you found a direct object, the verb is transitive.

   If the verb does not produce action, see if the answer to the questions *who* or *what* describes the subject; if so, then, you have a subject completer. If you found a subject completer (predicate noun, predicate pronoun, predicate adjective), the verb is intransitive.

4. Look for words, phrases, or clauses that modify parts of the sentence, and place them near the word(s) they modify. Refer to the examples in the discussion above. Following this exercise are web sites that offer instruction in and examples of diagramming.

D1 Diagramming—Exercises
(Page 213-215 Answers)

Diagram the following sentences. The "Answers" chapter, at the back of this guide, shows you diagrams for these sentences.

1. Birds fly.

2. Birds fly swiftly.

3. Blue birds fly swiftly.

4. Chubby, blue birds fly gracefully.

5. Chubby, blue birds fly gracefully through the trees.

6. The bird with the worm in her mouth is looking for her nest.

7. Her babies are eager for their dinner.

8. Nature's system of interdependency of creatures is intriguing.

9. Nature's order is brilliant.

10. Humans often create chaos.

Helpful Web Sites

Diagrams can accommodate sentences of all constructions and all lengths. To learn more about diagramming, consult the following web sources.

http://www.wisc-online.com/Objects/ViewObject.aspx?ID=WCN8207

http://www.german-latin-english.com/basicdiagrams.htm

http://grammar.ccc.commnet.edu/grammar/diagrams/diagrams.htm

http://grammar.ccc.commnet.edu/grammar/diagrams2/diagrams_frames.htm

http://grammar.ccc.commnet.edu/grammar/diagrams2/one_pager1.htm

Notes

Only in grammar can you be more than perfect.

—William Safire

Photo courtesy of Gabriel Flores

Remain focused on intention.

Chapter 9

Word Choices

Gender-Neutral Language

Language is ever evolving; new words are added to the dictionary, and existing words take on new definitions. Clearly, social and cultural changes influence language. One of the most striking changes in English vocabulary and grammar addresses gender-specific and gender-neutral language.

Nouns and Pronouns in Gender-Neutral Language

As pronouns such as he, him, and his have been used generically (to refer to both male and female), they are now considered incorrect by some grammarians because they identify one gender over another. (This is discussed in the section "Agreement of Pronoun and Antecedent.") This applies to compound words, too, such as council*man*, fire*man*, and *man*power.

Consider *members of the Council* rather than councilmen, *firefighter* rather than fireman, and *workers* or *staff* rather than manpower.

Rather than routinely referring to doctors as *men* or professors as *women,* consider writing in the plural and use *they.* (However, as discussed below, using the word *they* as a singular pronoun is gaining support of grammarians.)

Be aware of written and spoken language, which clearly reflects sexist thinking, as in the next sentences.

Oh, you have a new *doctor?* Who is *he?*

An *English professor* will always notice if *her* students speak well.

A *mathematics professor* will conduct *his* classes with precision.

In ever-increasing numbers, textbooks avoid gender-specific pronouns: he, she, him, her, his, and hers. In place of these singular pronouns, they use *they, themself,* and *theirself,* which are discussed below. (Using the plural *them* with the singular *they* goes against traditional grammar rules; in fact, *themself* was not recognized as a legitimate word. Similarly, *theirself* was not considered acceptable.)

Honorifics

Some etiquette writers consider the honorifics, or titles, Mrs. and Miss incorrect, as they are not marital-neutral as is Mr. *Miss* is used to identify a woman who is not married. *Mrs.* is used to refer to a married woman.

Before using the honorifics Mrs. or Miss, consider the marital-neutral Ms (which is not written with a period).

Agreement of Pronoun and Antecedent in Gender-Neutral Language

In some recently published textbooks, agreement of pronoun and antecedent as both singular or both plural has been put aside in favor of gender-neutral language. (The *student* will complete *his* homework tonight.) The authors of these textbooks explain that they want to avoid using gender-specific pronouns: he, she, him, her, his, and hers. In place of these singular pronouns, they use plural, gender-neutral pronouns to refer to singular nouns. (*The student* will complete *their* homework tonight.) The authors are replacing gender-specific with gender-neutral language.

An argument in favor of using *they* to refer to singular nouns draws on the fact that although writing may indicate he/she/it, the spoken language does not accept this inclusive reference. Consequently, *they* is used as a singular pronoun. In fact, following the more common use of *they* as plural, the words *themself* and *theirself* are creeping into modern speaking and writing and gaining legitimacy among scholars. This is to avoid gender-specific pronouns himself and herself.

The best *student* in my English class does *their* homework thoughtfully. (This sentence offers an example of a plural pronoun, *their*, referring to a singular subject, *student*.)

Indefinite pronouns (discussed in "Words") are more commonly used to reflect gender-neutral language.
I know that there must be *somebody* in the class who did *their* homework! (Here, again, is an example of a plural pronoun *their* referring to a singular pronoun *somebody*.)

Some traditional grammarians propose that if you choose to use gender-neutral language, consider writing in the plural; we, they, their, our, for example, are gender-neutral pronouns. By writing in the plural, you will be conforming to the standard (and traditional) rule of agreement of pronoun and antecedent while avoiding gender-specificity. However, if you do choose to refer to a singular noun with a plural pronoun, it is wise to alert the reader to your choice. If you are writing in an academic or professional setting, conform to the accepted style manual or confer with colleagues to determine acceptable style.

Wikipedia posts an illuminating discussion of the following words used as gender-neutral singular: *they, themself,* and *theirself.* You may read more about gender-neutral language on the web site http://en.wikipedia.org/wiki/ Singular_they.

Quirky Spelling

Too often, writers are stumped by homonyms, words that sound alike but are spelled differently and have different meanings. Following are some troublesome words; not all of them are homonyms. Once you read through the list, try the exercises to see if these words need more of your attention.

When you find yourself struggling for the correct word, search the computer for its correct use. For example, you can type **affect vs. effect**; several explanations will be offered. Read through them. See how several grammarians respond to the question; then choose the definition, the word, that is appropriate for your writing. Be consistent in how you use the terms. Remembering all the rules, structures, and tenses is not necessary. Knowing where to find the answers is vital. Writers' tools include a dictionary, a thesaurus, and a grammar reference book, either hard copy or electronic. *The GPS for Writing*, which is available in both hard copy and electronic form, can get you through just about all of the challenges that come up in your writing.

Spelling Rules—Just a Few Hints

Spelling rules abound. Some make sense and are easy to remember. I've enjoyed rhymes:
I before E
Except after C
Or when sounded like A
As in n*ei*ghbor and w*ei*gh.

This rule covers receive, deceive, perceive. I'm sure you can name others.

Look at the word **believe**. What do you see in the middle of the word? Do you see the word LIE? There it is, right in the middle of believe! Yikes!

Let's read the word **restaurant**. Pronounce it this way: rest-a-u-rant. Make it four syllables, and you're likely to spell it correctly.

The same goes for **together**. Think of to get her.

Just a few challenging words were cited to show you ways to remember their spelling. Consider words that you find especially difficult to spell correctly; everyone has them! Study the word specifically looking for ways to remember the spelling. First, write the words; then, study them in your special way of remembering.

You have heard people say, go to a dictionary if you can't spell a word. And you think, well, if I can look it up, I can spell it. This is not necessarily true. You may be able to sound out enough of the word to find the beginning letters to locate it in the dictionary. However, this requires your being able to identify **syllables**.

Can you find the beat in music? Can you tap your hand to the beat? Well, that's all you have to do to find syllables. Say the word slowly and deliberately. How many sounds do you hear? Tap your hand as you say the sounds. There you go! The number of times you tap your hands will tell you how many syllables the word has. When you look up a word that you're not sure how to spell, go one syllable at a time. Chances are that you will be able to find the word. Give it a try with the word **syllables**. Tap your hand. Did you tap three times—syl la ble?

It's reassuring to know that many computers and smartphones have voice-activated dictionaries that allow you to speak into the phone or computer, and the word will be found. Additionally, on command, these phones will confirm correct pronunciation.

Homonyms

Homonyms are words that sound alike but have different meanings. Dimitri, Elsa, and Peter had fun coming up with the following homonyms. I'll bet you can add to the list below.

Elsa Hadad
ad/add
by/buy/bye
hear/here
dear/deer
flour/flower
write/right
hour/our
mail/male
see/sea
present (time)/present (gift)
ant/aunt (There are a lot of ants in my aunt's house.)
sun/son (My son likes to play in the sun.)
rose/rows (The roses are in rows in my garden.)

Chein-Chang Peter Li
Peter chose to write sentences with homonyms.
  1. The maid made good tea this morning.
  2. When we meet, let me order meat.

3. That steel sea lion in the park is hard to steal, but it was stolen yesterday.
4. That suite is full of a sweet scent.
5. Today is a sunny Sunday, and we all will have a sundae.

Dimitri Vinson
mail/male
sail/sale
fare/fair
blue/blew
tail/tale
four/fore/for
see/sea
ad/add
so/sew
eight/ate
one/won
bee/be
pale/pail
there/their/they're
its/it's

Troublesome Words

The following list is by no means a complete list of troublesome words. These are words that often baffle writers; therefore, I've offered some tips that have seen me through my confusion about choosing the right word.

Accept/Except

Except means to **ex**clude. See the *ex* in both words? Everyone was invited **ex**cept (**ex**cluding) me.

If you **exclude** me, I know everyone in the class is invited **except** me.

Of course, if you invite me late, I will not **accept** your invitation.

Be certain to pronounce these words as they are spelled. **Ex** and **Ac** have different sounds. See if your computer or phone can pronounce the words. Listen carefully to the beginning sound of each of these words: except and accept.

Advice/Advise

Careful pronunciation of the ends of these two words will help you choose the correct one for your sentence. **Advise** is a verb, and **advice** is a noun.

When your adviser **advises** you about which word to choose, take the **advice**.

Affect/Effect

Most of the time, **affect** is a verb; therefore, it has a past tense: affected. **Affect** generally means to influence, to change something.

Effect is most often used as a noun meaning result. Remembering that **the** or **an** often precedes effect helps me to remember when to use **effect**.

My beautiful flowers are **affected** by the drought. (You see, **were affected/will be affected** ← tenses = verbs.)

My beautiful flowers show the **effects** of the drought. (**The** precedes **effect**.)

Another challenge comes during those *very rare* times when **affect** is a noun and **effect** is a verb.
Effect can be a verb, meaning to produce, to create.
Effect is a verb when it refers to something being brought about.

Do you really believe that consistent disciplinary actions **effect** change in children's behavior?
The doctor **effected** a cure for that ailment.

Affect can be a noun referring to feeling or emotion. However, **affect** is rarely used as a noun.

His **affect** was sincere when he came to apologize for forgetting her birthday.

Allot/A lot

Do you have **a lot** to do today? If so, you may want to **allot** some of the chores to me.

Did you know that those two words are spelled **a lot** and **allot**: one means *too much* and the other *to share* or *distribute*?

Already/All ready

Do you know the difference between the words **already** and **all ready**? Are you **ready** to go to the movies? If you can omit *all*, then write two words.

I have **ready** done my homework. What? That's not correct.
The words *all* and *ready* cannot be separated; therefore, write one word, *already*.

Already implies something completed. I have **already** done that.

Compose/Comprise

The word *of* is used with **composed.** The book is **composed of** many chapters. **Composed** refers to the whole product or concept which is made up of many parts.

The zoo **comprises** animals.
Comprise refers to the parts that make up the whole, and the whole is generally named before the parts. The play **comprises** many acts. Consider substituting the word includes for comprises.
The more frequently used of the two is **compose.**

Different From

Different from is much preferred over "different than."

Hear/Here

Do you see the **ear** in h**ear**? Does that help you to remember that **hear** has to do with your ear/hearing rather than the location **here**?

It's/Its

It's a lovely day in the neighborhood; everything is quiet. The apostrophe in **it's** indicates that a letter has been omitted, and the letter is **i**.

The lion was stalking **its** prey when the elephant threatened to attack. Here's one of the possessive words that does not require an apostrophe to show ownership. Like his, hers, ours, the possessive pronoun **its** has no apostrophe.

Laughter/Daughter

I love this next example. It shows how difficult English language pronunciation can be and how fascinating and unexpected connections between words can be.

Read this word, *laughter.*
Now, change the *L* to a *D*.
Look what word appears, **daughter**!
Isn't that lovely!
Well, it's lovely and confusing because two words that are spelled just about the same are pronounced so differently.

Find your own special ways that will help you to remember correct spelling.

Lie/Lay

Lie has two meanings: (1) to tell an untruth and (2) to rest. The third word discussed here is **lay** which means to place something . Let's start with a discussion of the word that means to tell an untruth because it's often less confusing than the other two words (which mean *to rest* and *to place*).

1. **Lie** is the present tense of the verb which means to tell an untruth, to make a false statement, and to deceive. Lie is a regular verb; its tenses are formed as most verbs.

Present	lie/lies
Past	lied
Future	will lie
Progressive	lying

The child lied when she said that she wasn't chewing gum.
The coach was lying about the team's success.

2. **Lie** is the present tense of the intransitive verb "to lie," which means to recline or rec**lie**ne. (Notice the word *lie* in the preceding misspelled "recline." Does that help you to remember what "to lie" means?) As an intransitive verb, **lie** is not followed by an object.

   The baby **lies** quietly in her crib and watches the sunbeams play on the ceiling.

3. **Lay** is the present tense of the transitive verb "to lay," which means to place something or to p**lay**ce something. (Notice the word "lay" in the preceding word? I deliberately misspelled "place" to help you understand that **lay** means to place something. Please, **lay** the baby in the crib.) Does that help you to remember what "to lay" means? As a transitive verb, "to lay" is followed by a direct object.

   Please, Sonia, **lay** the dishes on the table.
   "Dishes" is the direct object of "lay."

Let me show you how the irregular verbs "to lie" and "to lay" are formed.

	To lie (intransitive)	To lay (transitive)
Present	lie	lay
Past	lay	laid
Future	will lie	will lay
Present perfect	have lain	have laid
Past perfect	had lain	had laid
Future perfect	will have lain	will have laid
Present progressive	is/are lying	is/are laying
Past progressive	was/were lying	was/were laying
Future progressive	will be lying	will be laying
Present perfect progressive	have/has been lying	have/has been laying
Past perfect progressive	had been lying	had been laying
Future perfect progressive	will have been lying	will have been laying

Here are several examples of the correct use of lie and lay.
Remember to lie = to recline (intransitive verb)
        to lay = to place something (transitive verb)
            takes a direct object

Examples:

to lie—to recline

Present—The baby now **lies** in the crib quietly at night.

Past—The baby **lay** in the crib quietly last night.

Future—The baby **will lie** in the crib until she falls asleep.

Present progressive—The baby **is lying** in the crib quietly.

Present Perfect—The baby **has lain** quietly in the crib since finishing her bottle.

Present Perfect Progressive—The baby **has been lying** in the crib with her cuddly toy.

to lay—to place (place something, the direct object)

Present—Mom **lays** the baby in the crib after the baby plays.

Past—Mom **laid** the baby in the crib.

Future—Mom **will lay** the baby in the crib after the baby's bath.

Present Progressive—Mom **is laying** the baby next to the cuddly toys.

Present Perfect—Mom **has laid** the baby in the crib since the baby finished eating.

Present Perfect Progressive—Mom **has been laying** cuddly toys in the baby's crib.

Mom **will lie** down after she **lays** the baby in the crib for the night.

Have some fun with this example of using "to lay" (place), ""to lie," (tell an untruth), and "to lie," (to rest).

> While laying the plate on the table, he lied to his brother about lying down for a nap in the afternoon.

That/Which/Who

Use the word **that** for animals, people, things without specific names.
She wanted a dog **that** would be comfortable in a small apartment.

Use **which** only for animals and things—not people.
The SUV, **which** seats six passengers comfortably, is expensive.

Use **who** for people and animals with specific names.
My favorite professor, Dr. Taylor, **who** has been teaching for forty years, just retired.

Then/Than

Then refers to time. See the **e** in **then** and the **e** in time.
I will go to the movies**; then**, I'll have dinner.
Than refers to comparison or contrast. See the **a** in **than** and the **a** in comparison and contrast.

When pronouncing both **then** and **than**, listen to the difference. Make the word **then** rhyme with hen and **than** rhyme with van**.**

There/They're/Their

W*here* do you want to put the book?
Do you want to put the book **here**?
No, put it *there*!
Notice the word **here** in each of the examples above. T**here**, **here**, and w**here** refer to place. Will this help you to remember the correct spelling of **there**?

Wherever the word *his* can be used, so can the word *their* be used; they both show possession or ownership. And, they both have the letter **i**. That may help you to remember; the letter **i** is the secret!

Andrew asked the guys if he could borrow (there/they're/their) scuba equipment for the dive.
Both *his* and *their* work in this sentence. Therefore, because you need the plural to agree with "guys," you would choose **their**.

The other homonym is **they're**. This is a contraction for the words **they are.** When we join words and omit letters, the apostrophe is placed where the letters are omitted. The letter **a** is omitted from **they are**. Therefore, the apostrophe is placed where the letter **a** would have been.

Thought/Taught

Pronunciation is the key to understanding these two words. They are both part tense verbs. When pronouncing them, watch the initial sounds: "th" and "t."

Thought is the past tense of think.
Gee, I **thought** you'd like to have dinner with me.

Taught is the past tense of teach.
Yesterday, I **taught** the students about verbs.

Where/Wear

These words sound alike (homonyms), but their meanings are different. Above, we discussed **there, here, where**. All of these words have to do with place. Each of these words includes the word **here**. Remember the **here** in w**here** and in t**here.**

> **here** = place
> w**here** = place
> t**here** = place

This might help: *where* should I put the book? Put it *here*? **T***here*? No, *here*.

Be sure to **wear** your clean and pressed jeans to the dance tomorrow night. A synonym for wear is "to clothe," and the definition would be *to have on the body*. There are other definitions for **wear**; however, the one that often causes problems has to do with clothing. A dictionary is the best source for assistance.

Who/Whom

Since **who** is used for the subject of a sentence and **whom** is used for objects (objective-case pronoun), here's an easy way to remember when to use **who** and **whom**.

Use **who** whenever a substitution of **he** sounds right.
Use **whom** whenever a substitution of **him** sounds right.
Think of the **m** in him and the **m** in **whom**, and you're set!

You went to the party with **who**? **whom**? You went to the party with **whom**?
You went to the party with **he**? **him**? You went to the party with **him**.

Which sounds right?
You went to the party with **him**. Yes, this is correct.
Therefore, you can safely say:
You went to the party with **whom**?

Here are two more examples:

He is a teacher (**who/whom**) took the students on a field trip.
> He took the students on a field trip.
> **Who** took the students on a field trip?
> He did, not him did!
> Who is the correct choice.
> He is the teacher who took the students on a field trip.

She is the woman (**who/whom**) Joe hired.
> **Who** did Joe hire?
> Joe hired her.
> Use **whom** when her/him works.
> The answer is **whom**.
> She is the woman **whom** Joe hired.

Who's/Whose

Who's is a contraction for "who is." The apostrophe is placed where the letter is missing; the missing letter is **i**.
I hear the doorbell ringing; **who's** there?

Whose refers to ownership; it refers to possession.
Whose basketball is that?

CW1 Word Choices—Exercises
(Page 211 Answers)

Choose the correct word in 1-10. In 11-18, correct the errors in all the sentences. Check your answers to see if you have mastered these challenges.

1. The puppy wildly chases (it's/its) tail.

2. Watching kittens play with (their/they're/there) catnip toys is a joy.

3. I would love to have (allot/a lot) of dogs, but my apartment is (too/to/two) small.

4. When my homework is completed, I will be (already/all ready) to walk your dog.

5. Will the rain (affect/effect) whether the dog wants to go out?

6. Let's walk the dog; (than/then), we can go for ice cream.

7. (Who's/whose) dog was barking all night?

8. I can't (except/accept/expect) a puppy because I just don't have time to care for it.

9. You've given me (advise/advice), but (its/it's) not working for me; I can't have a pet at this time.

10. Coming home from a stressful day at work, (than/then) taking the dog for a walk is a lovely way to calm down and leave the stress behind rather (then/than) rushing to prepare for the next day and not clearing your mind.

Lori wrote about tending her garden. (Correct the errors in 11-18.)

11. I am a early riser.

12. One of the first things I due when I wake up in the morning is water my garden.

13. I begin with the window boxes on the west side of the house and, than, work my way over to the mixed perennial beds in the front of the house.

14. Once a week, if it is real hot, I'll water the hedges surrounding the beds.

15. This entire process can take over a hour, but I don't mine.

16. I prefer using an hand-held wand too just turning on an sprinkler.

17. I enjoy being in the garden early in the mourning when its quite and still.

18. Tending my garden gives me time to think before I start my day.

Specific Challenges in Word Choice and Placement

When preparing this grammar guide, I asked colleagues if their students in ESL, developmental, and advanced writing courses had specific writing challenges that were especially difficult to change. Most of the concerns raised are addressed in this guide; however, a few remain open for discussion.

Challenge #1

Annette's students have a difficult time when they begin sentences with prepositional phrases. They seem to confuse the object of the prepositional phrase with the subject of the sentence. The subject of the sentence is missing. Therefore, we don't have CVS; we don't have a sentence. To avoid this error, rework the sentence so that it does not begin with a prepositional phrase. Or, identify a subject, and place it before the verb.

Here's the example with the error.
In Sylvia Plath's poem, "Daddy," deals with her feelings of resentment toward her father.

Every sentence must have **CVS**—a **c**omplete thought, a **v**erb, and a **s**ubject. The verb in the example above is **deals.** What's the subject? To find the subject of the verb, ask **who** or **what + verb**. Therefore, we ask **who** or **what deals**? Does "Daddy," the name of the poem deal?

"Daddy" deals with her feelings? No, "Daddy" is the name of the poem. The title of the poem is not dealing with her feelings. So, who deals with her feelings of resentment toward her father? The author of the poem, Sylvia Plath, deals with her feelings of resentment. The subject of the sentence, the person whom the verb is telling about, needs to be stated.

Here's the example with the correction.
   "Sylvia Plath's poem 'Daddy' deals with her feelings of resentment
      toward her father."

All writing must be carefully **proofread** with thoughtful attention to the words, to the sentences, and to the paragraphs. Writing is a complex process, and proofreading is difficult because our eyes play tricks on us. We think we've written very clearly; however, when proofreading, we'll find that improvements can be made.

Reading aloud may help to identify clumsy and incorrect word usage, grammar, and sentence structure.

Challenge #2

Thomas said that his advanced ESL students have difficulty with different uses of -ing words and auxiliary verbs (helping verbs).

This problem may stem from a lack of familiarity or understanding of the progressive tenses; for example, consider I am going, I had been going, I will have been going. (Verb tenses are discussed in the chapter "Word.")

"I am go to school?" is incorrect. This may be where the ESL students are having difficulty. Conjugating verbs through all the twelve tenses is a way to approach this problem. Additionally, reviewing *forms* of verbs—present form, past form, past participle form—will be helpful. It's important to understand that **helping verbs** are essential in communicating time/tense. (Helping verbs are discussed in "Words.")

Defining **verbs** as **action words** is not always reliable. Consider defining verbs as words that tell *time*, that is, *tense*. The verb is the word in the sentence that can be changed to indicate past or future or present. Once the writer understands that concept, the importance of the helping verb will be realized and, hopefully, used. (Verbs are discussed in detail in "Words.")

The grocer ran after me with my change.
The grocer will run
The grocer runs

The grocer running after me with my change ← What is the tense of this phrase?

The **helping verb** will give the *tense*. *Running* does not carry tense.

Note that in the following sentences that "running" stays the same while the tense changes. The tense changes because the **helping verbs** indicate the tense.

The grocer <u>was running.</u>
The grocer <u>has been running.</u>
The grocer <u>will have run.</u>

Challenge #3

Mária reports that her students use the awkward phrase "in which."

Here's an example with an error.
The speech by Martin Luther King, in which I just read, is called "I Have a Dream."
A correction could be—The speech I just read by Martin Luther King is called "I Have a Dream."

When misplaced, the phrase "in which" creates awkward writing. The objects of prepositional phrases cannot be the subjects of sentences. All verbs must express tense/time. Correct the sentences in C2 Word Choices—Exercises.

CW2 Word Choices—Exercises
(Page 212 Answers)

Sentences in the following exercise are to be corrected for the three challenges just identified: missing subject, incorrect verb form, and the awkward phrase "in which." Write the sentence correctly in the lines provided. If you have difficulty rewording these sentences, read them aloud. Hearing them just might be what you need to make appropriate corrections. Check your answers.

1. My son likes California, *in which* he says is a dreamland.

   _____

2. Martin Luther King, Jr. wants his children to enjoy a life *in which* he longed for himself.

   _____

3. President Obama gives a speech, one *in which* motivates an entire nation to act.

   _____

4. Sam *was go* to India to study yoga.

_____

5. In *The New York Times* article "NYC Firemen are Heroes," reports on three huge fires in one night. (Where's the subject?)

_____

CW3 Word Choices—Exercises
(Page 212 Answers)

Find ten errors in the following sentences: spelling, homonyms, tense.

Basketball Is My Game by Mario Leopold

1. My favorite basketball teem is the New York Knicks.

2. I played basketball at age eleven.

3. I played in the Nike Swish Tournament in 2006; we loss in the playoffs.

4. My love fore the game growed as a I got older.

5. I have seven basketball trofees.

6. My favorite movie are "He Got Game," a flim about basketball.

7. I gone as far as Montreal four a basketball game.

8. Montreal has alot of ball players from many cultures.

9. My favorite basketball player is Derrick Rose.

10. Derrick Rose plays for the Chicago Bulls NBA team.

Building Vocabulary

Studying prefixes, suffixes, and root words is an effective way to increase vocabulary. Both prefixes and suffixes are letters added to words that change the meaning of the words.

Many workbooks list common prefixes, including "a," "un," "dis," which often mean "not," and "anti" (against), "auto" (self).

typical	*a*typical
wrap	*un*wrap
ability	*dis*ability
social	*anti*social
biography	*auto*biography

Suffixes are letters added to the ends of words. These include "able" (capable of being), "er/or" (one who), and "dom" (state of).

love	lov*able*
teach	teach*er*
free	free*dom*

Root words are the base words that prefixes and suffixes are attached to.
Look at the word "appoint."
Add a prefix, and the word becomes "disappoint."
Add a suffix, and the word becomes "appointment."

Take the root word "teach."
Add a suffix, and the word becomes "teacher."

Studying root words, suffixes, and prefixes is the quickest way to increase vocabulary and fine-tune spelling.

Dictionaries, Wikipedia, and other electronic word-reference guides are essential tools for writers. Words not only have basic definitions, which is the **denotation** of the word, but also words carry **connotations**, shades of meaning often taken from experience.

In this sentence, we see the **denotation** of "wolf."
A *wolf* is a large, carnivorous mammal that usually hunts in packs and lives in areas that are sparsely populated.

In this sentence, we read the **connotation** of "wolf."
That man is a terrible *wolf*; I tell my girlfriends to stay away from him.
In this sentence, "wolf" is used informally to refer to a man who makes unwanted advances to many women.

This short passage about vocabulary building is meant to call your attention to the construction of words. Study prefixes, suffixes, and the roots of words, and your vocabulary will increase rapidly.

Helpful Web Sites

http://virtualsalt.com/vocablst.htm

http://www.testprepreview.com/prefixes_suffixes.htm

http://www.uefap.com/vocab/build/building.htm

http://www.drgrammar.org/frequently-asked-questions

http://jerz.setonhill.edu/writing/grammar-and-syntax/gender-neutral-language/

Notes

Don't use words too big for the subject. Don't say infinitely when you mean very; otherwise you'll have no word left when you want to talk about something really infinite.

—C. S. Lewis

_____

_____

_____

_____

_____

_____

_____

_____

_____

_____

_____

_____

_____

_____

_____

_____

Chapter 10

Facing the Blank Page—The Composing Process

Now, let's write!

Chapters 2-9 focus on the mechanics of writing and offer instruction, review, exercises with answers, and web sites for further explanation and practice. The study of grammar, punctuation, and structure may be fun, for some, by itself; however, for most people, it's the means to the end: composing an effective piece of writing. Grammar, punctuation, and sentence structure provide the support, the foundation for writing. Being able to correctly use words to form engaging sentences is imperative to successful communication. Knowing that you have mastered the basic structures will give you confidence in your writing, for you will, in fact, be able to proofread effectively not just for content but also for mechanical correctness to confirm that your writing fulfills your intention. The first nine chapters in *The GPS* give you the foundation and support to move ahead into the composing process.

Fear of Writing

I know what it's like to stare at a clean and white sheet of paper—a beautiful blank piece of paper; but the challenge of putting words that make sense onto that paper gradually becomes terrifying. Not only must these words make sense, but also they must be spelled correctly and grouped logically to communicate engaging ideas clearly. A frequent response to this task is paralysis: the inability to think of anything to say; the mind goes blank. Some people begin to sweat; their foreheads become moist; their palms become damp, perhaps, their hands shake. There are many physical manifestations of this fear of writing. Sometimes, the fear comes from previous unpleasant experiences with writing. Sometimes, it comes from the belief that you just have nothing worthwhile to say. Sometimes, it comes from the awareness that the basic skills of spelling, grammar, punctuation, and sentence structure are just mysteries. If you suffer from writer's block, paralysis, or freeze, you may find it useful to consider what may be causing these terribly unpleasant feelings.

Reality Checks

Perhaps, some reality checking can assuage your feelings of not being up to the task of writing. Do you feel confident that you know the basic rules governing correct writing? Have you completed most of the work in the preceding chapters? Do you understand the mechanics of writing as presented in *The GPS*? If you do not, then give yourself a gift; go back and review those chapters until you feel good knowing that you have a better understanding of these concepts. Becoming more familiar with the material in this text will help you to use this information as a reference to guide you when you have specific questions. You don't have to keep all the information in your head. As explained in the introduction to *The GPS*, knowing what questions to ask will help you find the answers to your composing, editing, and revising challenges. It may seem counter-intuitive, but the more familiar you are with the mechanics of writing, the more specific your questions can be; consequently, you will be more likely to find the answers.

Do you find you have nothing to write about? Reading the hard or ecopy of newspapers, books, magazines, or comic books, for example, will fill your mind with ideas that can inform your writing. Even information gleaned from conversations may effectively contribute to your compositions. Take time to sincerely reflect on your life experiences; it's my belief that you will find at least several very important events in your life that significantly affected you. It's likely that others have had similar experiences, so if you were to write about those events, your reader will be able to identify with your message and appreciate your perspective.

It's so important that you value all the information that you have accumulated throughout your lifetime no matter how young or old you are. Your preferences for music and fashion and your experiences of family life have the potential to enrich your writing. It's a matter of valuing your perspective, your vision, and your interpretation of reality. Trusting that your thoughts are worthwhile, believing that your ideas are interesting to other people, being confident that you can communicate these ideas in a way that will engage another person, that's all very scary. Writing is scary, but there are some things we can do to help us *take the dive*!

Photo courtesy of Andy Feder

Taking the dive and trusting that you can come through the journey successfully requires courage, confidence, and skill.

Proofreading

When you write, do you very carefully proofread your work? Several methods of proofreading are discussed in Chapter 2; review them. No writer can expect to have words, paragraphs, or pages tumble out and make perfect sense. Writing is a continuous process of rereading, revising, and rewriting. Many writers discover their ideas as they write; consequently, they must go back to the beginning of their work to rephrase, reorder, as well as delete and add ideas. Often we stray from the intention we set out to accomplish. Other ideas enter our minds and, understandably, distract us. These ideas may seem more engaging than the idea we initially set out to write about.

Photo courtesy of Andy Feder

Give yourself time to see the possibilities that exist.

Proofreading will help us discover if we have gone astray and help us get back to our intention. Not only do we want the content to be logically developed and clearly understood, but also we want it to be engaging. For example, to draw the reader into our work, we need to be concerned about pace, tempo, and word choice. Here's where we need to look at the vocabulary and stretch to find more effective choices; we need to vary the sentence types, kinds, and length to create an engaging rhythm, a sense of urgency, or a flow of descriptions.

Moving Into the Composing Process

We study grammar, punctuation, and structure in *The GPS for Writing* because we're concerned about communicating as effectively as possible in writing. Additionally, we want to know how to create writing that engages the reader. Some of us already write well and would like to know what exactly makes our writing successful. Some of us want to write well, so we need to look at the composing process from the ground up.

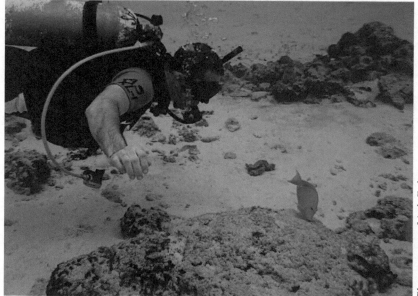

Photo courtesy of Andy Feder

Consider which ideas you would like to follow; consider those you can most easily and comfortably pursue.

In fact, both experienced writers as well as beginning writers will benefit from studying the composing process. This study offers an opportunity to reflect on logical development of ideas, precise word selection, varying sentence kinds and patterns, and effective paragraphing: the elements that create well-written compositions. In fact, I would like to offer an acronym to help you remember the essential components of effective writing: CUE. C is for **coherence**; U is for **unity**, and E is for **emphasis**. These terms are explained below.

As a metaphor for the study of creating an effective composition, let's think about scuba diving, yes, deep-sea diving. I like this concept; even if you haven't gone scuba diving (as I haven't), you can visualize the bottom of the sea in all its darkness. And, you are aware that as you move closer to the surface, light begins to penetrate the water. Ultimately, you reach through the water into sunlight! During the dive, you see brilliantly colored fish; magnificently twisted opaque, translucent, and transparent mollusks; deep green, tangled sea grass; an abundance of extraordinary, engaging, and distracting sites. Yet, you need to focus on your mission to be assured of adequate oxygen and light to complete your underwater journey.

Photo courtesy of Andy Feder

You really must dive right into the topic. When you look around, your thoughts might be murky, but you need to trust that eventually you will find your way. Give thoughtful consideration to all that floats through your mind.

Photo courtesy of Andy Feder

Take time to explore, brainstorm, or cluster your thoughts because there are so many ideas floating around.

Brainstorming

While writing, we are often distracted by insights our minds want to follow; however, we need to stay focused on the message we want to communicate. Clearly, it's necessary to brainstorm and to consider all ideas that might help us convey our thoughts. We need to explore the terrain, see all the possibilities from our unique perspective before we hone in on a strategy for achieving our objective. We can't let our ideas get muddled by the multitude of marvelous distractions. We must keep reminding ourselves to come back to the topic, to our intention.

Photo courtesy of Andy Feder

Continue exploring until you find ideas that intrigue you and that you know enough about to create an engaging composition.

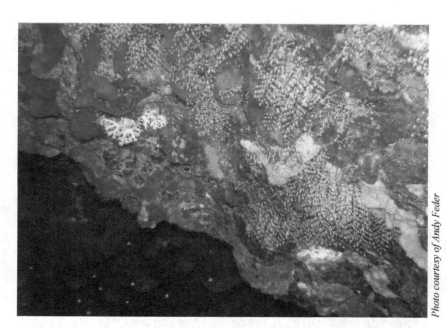

Photo courtesy of Andy Feder

Allow yourself to be open to new ideas; allow your mind to be free of fears and constraints. Trust in your ability to observe, feel, interpret, and record.

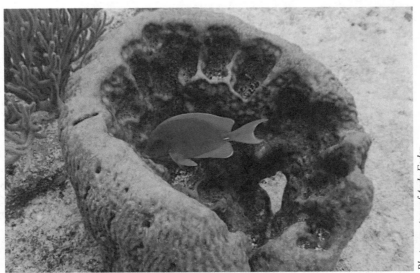

Photo courtesy of Andy Feder

Once you think you have found the idea you would like to develop, give yourself time to consider how you might focus on this topic. Think about the five important questions that need to be answered in all writing: who, how, why, when, and where.

C = Coherence

One way to help us remain on target is to write an **outline**. Some people prefer to create an outline prior to writing; others prefer to write several paragraphs and then see how and if the ideas can work into an outline. There are other writers who put all of their ideas on paper, then, write an outline to confirm or, if necessary, reorder ideas to create a logical sequence of development. The extraneous ideas need to be discarded for the sake of clear communication. Sometimes, we think we have found our objective for writing, but when we begin to write about it, we get stumped. We run out of ideas. Rather than struggling and staying with an idea that seems to fall flat, move on to other ideas.

Photo courtesy of Andy Feder

Times will occur when ideas seem exciting and worth writing about, but when we start the process, we quickly become stumped. We need to recognize that when the thoughts stop coming and we've reached the point where we have nothing else to say, it's time to explore other perspectives or other topics. We need to look at the ideas that come up during the brainstorming stage or when we are clustering ideas.

U = Unity

Writing needs to be clear. The reader needs to be able to easily see the connection between ideas. There are several ways to achieve clarity. We need to be aware of **logical development** of ideas. **Tense consistency** is essential for writing to be logically developed and to help the reader follow the message. Transitional words, phrases, and clauses keep ideas connected.

Remember FITCHMINT, which is discussed in Chapter 6, "Sentence Patterns?" FITCHMINT is an acronym for conjunctive adverbs that are used to create compound sentences. These words also serve extremely effectively as transitional words. Let me remind you: furthermore, indeed, therefore, consequently, however, moreover, in fact, nevertheless, then. Can you see how these words help to connect ideas?

Photo courtesy of Andy Feder

You may try several ideas before you find the one that works for you. That's the benefit of brainstorming or clustering ideas. Both methods of generating ideas will help you to see which topics work best for you.

E = Emphasis

Sensitivity to tone will encourage the reader to be engaged. We want to draw the reader in to keep the reader's interest. Selecting words carefully will either attract the reader or may create distance. Consider if you want to write in first, second, or third person and the effects of your choices. What tense works best for your subject matter? The decisions you make will help you to communicate effectively the points that you want the reader to remember. Staying focused and emphasizing specific ideas through sentence patterns, sentence types, and word choices will enable the reader to understand your message.

Photo courtesy of Andy Feder

It may happen that as you're writing, you feel as if you've lost focus. It may be that another idea has pushed itself forward in your mind. This may create confusion, but stay with it. The bubbles will clear, and the focus will become obvious as you continue writing, proofreading, editing, and revising.

Photo courtesy of Andy Feder

Aha! Now, I've got it! It's crystal clear.

CUE = Coherence, Unity, and Emphasis

When you have found the words and the structures that succinctly, effectively, and most successfully engage the reader, you'll know it. You'll be able to test the logical development of the ideas by checking the introductory paragraph against the concluding paragraph. You will be able to identify the main idea (topic sentence) of each body paragraph (whether stated or implied) and see that each topic sentence supports your thesis: the intention of your writing. You will be able to read the topic sentence (or identify the main idea if implied rather than stated) and follow the development, the growth, and yes, the progression of your idea.

If the thread of the idea is lost between paragraphs, you will need to reconstruct your plan. After all, our goal is to communicate effectively. In effective communication, it's necessary to lead the reader step-by-step through the unfolding of your ideas. Careful proofreading will help you to confirm that you have arranged your words, sentences, and paragraphs logically; consequently, you will be assured that your intention for your writing is crystal clear to the reader.

Once the idea becomes clear and the development of the idea starts to flow, you can feel yourself moving from the bubbles and the murkiness toward the light.

Photo courtesy of Andy Feder

When you are ready to complete your writing, you will have this wonderful feeling, just like the diver who sees the light upon ascending to the surface! This is a journey worth taking.

As you make your ascent—as you complete your final proofreading, you will see that all the distracting ideas and all the darkness and confusion have disappeared; your work will be thoroughly engaging and well written. You will feel just like the deep-sea divers when they are completing the dive and are ready to break through the water into the light!

Photo courtesy of Gabriel Flores

Success! You did it! You effectively brought all the essential tools together to achieve your goal!

Helpful Web Sites

http://owl.english.purdue.edu/owl/resource/587/1/

http://webtech.kennesaw.edu/jcheek4/writing.htm

http://writesite.cuny.edu/

http://voices.yahoo.com/how-write-composition-2245472.html

Chapter 11

The GPS for Writing

GPS

*Active route
Passive route* 09:16 14ᴍᴘʜ

GRAMMAR · PUNCTUATION · SENTENCE STRUCTURE

Structuring an Essay—in Brief

All writing consists of an introductory paragraph, body paragraphs, and a concluding paragraph. Whether you're writing a letter, a 500-word report, a 3,000-word research paper, an article for publication, or, in fact, a speech, yes, all writing has a clear introduction, body, and conclusion. (Speeches also have the same structure; in *The GPS,* we will focus on expository writing.)

INTRODUCTION

There may be many   BODY
more *body* paragraphs
depending on the purpose   BODY
of the writing.

BODY

CONCLUSION

A New Paragraph

When beginning a new paragraph, indent five spaces. (Generally, the TAB key will get you to where you need to be.) If you prefer not to indent, skip a line between paragraphs. Indentation and skipping a line when beginning a new paragraph are important signals to the reader that you will be discussing another idea, related to the thesis, of course, but an idea different from the previous paragraph.

Every paragraph develops one main idea. When you are finished discussing that idea, move to another paragraph (by indenting or double space between lines) for the next idea. The main idea sentence is called the **topic sentence**. The sentence that controls the entire composition is called the **thesis statement.** (A multi-paragraph piece of writing can be called a composition, theme, essay, thesis.)

The Purpose of the Introduction

The purpose of the introduction is to give the readers an idea of what you will be writing about. Some people say, "the introduction is where you tell them what you're going to tell them; the body is where you tell them, and the conclusion is where you tell them what you've told them."

The Purpose of the Body Paragraphs

The body paragraphs fully discuss the main idea, also known as the thesis statement. Body paragraphs explain or support your main idea. Each body paragraph has its own topic sentence, and that sentence will contain key words that reveal the support for and refer back to the thesis statement.

An essay generally has a minimum of three body paragraphs. Here are examples of how to develop them.

Body Paragraph #1: Begin with **one good reason** to support your thesis—your main idea. Be sure to give specific examples to back up this reason. Consider including a quotation.

Body Paragraph #2: Begin this paragraph with **another good reason** why the reader should agree with your thesis. Again, be sure to give specific examples, so the reader can fully understand why you are taking the position expressed in your thesis. Consider including a paraphrase or summary of a book or an article from a magazine or newspaper. Refer to information from a web site or a film.

Body Paragraph #3: Begin this paragraph with yet **another good reason** why the reader should agree with your opinion about the main idea. Again, be sure to give specific examples either from your readings, a friend's experience, or from your life experiences to back up your reason. An anecdote could, certainly, provide personal and intriguing information. Consider quoting from sources that you have read or heard to give credence to your position.

The Purpose of the Concluding Paragraph

The conclusion will restate the main idea which is the thesis statement that is expressed in the introductory paragraph and discussed in the body paragraphs. You may summarize the topic sentences from the body paragraphs. You may offer an opinion that differs from the position you supported to identify its weaknesses, but don't spend much time on this, for your purpose is to conclude this piece of writing. You don't want to introduce new ideas and leave the reader hanging.

The conclusion should bring your ideas to a satisfying end. You may want to end with a question; however, it should be directly related to the thesis statement, and the answer would be within your essay, so in actuality, you're not introducing anything new. You're asking the reader to rethink the ideas presented in your paper.

Overall Structure of a Composition

One of my students said that the structure of an essay is like a hamburger on a bun. The top of the hamburger bun states the main idea; the bottom of the bun echoes the main idea, and the hamburger is the juicy meat—the body!

Transition Between Sentences and Paragraphs

Remember the FITCHMINT words in Chapter 6? They are great transitional words between sentences and between paragraphs, as are the words just below this paragraph. If you can join two paragraphs with transitional words, that would be excellent! Transitional words show relationships between ideas whether within a sentence, between sentences, or between paragraphs. They show, for example, cause and effect; they show that something is a result of something else.

Examples of transitional words include the following:

Above all	In other words
Afterward	In spite of
Although	On the contrary
As an illustration	Simultaneously
Certainly	To illustrate

Ending a paragraph with a hint at what's coming in the next paragraph is very effective. Similarly, starting a paragraph with an echo of what came before provides great transition; it helps the reader to move easily between paragraphs, that is, between your ideas.

Title

A title is very helpful to the reader. It gives the reader an idea of what the writing is about. The title should be short and should catch the reader's interest. Your original title is not underlined and does not have quotation marks. (See Chapter 7 for information about when to capitalize words in titles.) The first and last words of the title are always capitalized as are other important words, which means that words like **a, an, the,** and **prepositions** that are not the first or last words in the title are, generally, not capitalized.

Suggestion

In Chapter 10, I discussed CUE: coherence, unity, emphasis: essential elements of effective writing. Clear thesis statements and topic sentences are vital for effective writing. Identifying them throughout your paper will help you to confirm that your work is logically developed. If you haven't already read Chapter 10, take some time now because it will help you to understand the importance of logical structure, full and focused development, and well thought-out ideas.

Chapter 12

Proofreading Marks

All style manuals have their own set of proofreading marks. They cover similar topics. Here is a list of common errors and abbreviations to indicate those errors. Refer to the Index for a quick way to locate explanations of all the words listed below.

Grammar (Words)

adj/adv	adjective and/or adverb incorrectly used
dm	dangling modifier
mm	misplaced modifier
pc	pronoun case
pro/ant agr	pronoun/antecedent agreement
shift P	shift in person
shift T	shift in tense
sp	spelling error
s/p	singular/plural
s/v agr	subject/verb agreement
vt	verb tense
we	word ending (plural or tense)

Punctuation

(')	apostrophe
B	**bold** needed
cap	capitalization
(,)	comma
(:)	colon
(—)	em dash

(–)	en dash
(!)	exclamation mark
(-)	hyphen
∧	insert words (carat)
i	*italics* needed
(.)	period
(?)	question mark
" "	quotation marks (double)
' '	quotation marks (single)
(;)	semi-colon
U	underline needed

Sentence Structure

cs	comma splice
frag	fragment
//	parallel structure
ro	run on/fused sentences

Composing Skills

awk	sentences are awkward or wordy
B	body paragraphs (B1, B2, etc.) need fuller development
C	concluding paragraph is not satisfying
coh	coherence (scattered ideas)
del	delete material
ed	edit
Fi	faulty inference
I	introductory paragraph inadequate
isi	inadequate supporting ideas
L	logical development
¶	paragraph
rep	repetitive
rev	revise
> <	spacing
T	title needed
tu	thesis unclear
ts	topic sentence, main idea of paragraph unclear
ww	wrong word (homonyms, connotation, denotation)

Notes

To write well, express yourself like the common people, but think like a wise man.

—Aristotle

Photo courtesy of Andy Feder

Make choices very thoughtfully.

Chapter 13

Glossary in Brief: *GPS for Writing*

Clauses are groups of words that include a subject and a verb.
A clause can be independent or dependent.
<u>Because I love you</u>, I will bring you chocolate candy.
Dependent clause (subordinate clause)—Because I love you
Independent clause—I will bring you chocolate candy

Conjunctions join words, phrases, and clauses.
I love you, <u>so</u> I will bring you chocolate candy.
I love you; <u>therefore</u>, I will bring you chocolate candy.
I will bring you chocolate candy <u>and</u> wine <u>because</u> I love you.
<u>Neither</u> chocolate candy <u>nor</u> wine are adequate in expressing
my appreciation, <u>but</u> I hope you will enjoy them.

Modifiers are adjectives and adverbs (words, phrases, and clauses)
that describe nouns, pronouns, adjectives, and adverbs.
My <u>undying</u> love for you <u>always</u> leaves me <u>achingly</u> wanting
to see you.
adjective—undying
always—adverb
achingly—adverb

Objects complete the meaning of words or phrases.
I bought you a <u>box</u> of <u>chocolates,</u> but they melted in my
<u>backpack</u>!
direct object—box
indirect object—you
objects of prepositions—chocolates and backpack

Phrases are groups of words that go together and do not include both a subject and a verb.
"Next time," she said, "buy me cupcakes and don't put them into your backpack!"
prepositional phrase—into your backpack

Predicates are the word(s) that reveal the tense and (often) action in the sentence. In some texts, the **predicate** includes the verb and its modifiers.
I will be studying all night and eating the melted chocolates, so I'll be up if you call really late.
Every clause has a verb/predicate whether an independent or dependent clause.

Subjects of sentences are the word(s) that the sentence is discussing.
My stomach is killing me because I finished the entire box of candy!
Each clause has a subject.

Subject Completer (subject complement) is a noun, pronoun, or adjective following an intransitive verb.
The book is fascinating.
subject completer—fascinating\
The author of this book is I.
subject completer—I

Thesis Statement—the main idea, the controlling idea of an essay or a composition or a theme

Topic Sentence—the central idea of a paragraph and may appear any place in the paragraph or may be implied

Verb, the word used interchangeably with **predicate,** indicates the tense in the sentence. In some texts, the word predicate includes the verb and its modifiers, the complete verb.

Verbals are forms of verbs used as nouns or adjectives. They are infinitives, participles, and gerunds.
Gerund (noun)—OK, eating chocolates is my favorite thing!
Participle (adjective)—I even love melted chocolates.
Infinitive (noun)—Do you like to eat chocolates, too?

Notes

Words, once they are printed, have a life of their own.

—Carol Burnett

Notes

Language is the blood of the soul into which thoughts run and out of which they grow.

—Oliver Wendell Holmes

_____

_____

_____

_____

_____

_____

_____

_____

_____

_____

_____

_____

_____

_____

_____

_____

Chapter 14

Pre-Test Exercises and Answers

Pre-Test Exercises
(Page 186 Answers)

Here are sentences to help you assess your knowledge of basic grammar. You may complete all of the exercises or choose what interests you at this time. The answers for this pre-test are at the end of this chapter. The point value for each exercise is written next to the title. The total number of points is 100.

I. WORDS (20)
(page 186 answers)

Identify the parts of speech of the words underlined.

1. The <u>extremely</u> <u>hot</u> sun <u>is burning</u> everyone who is sitting <u>on</u> the beach.

2. Sunscreen and <u>umbrellas</u> are not effective against the <u>skin-damaging</u> rays because the sun <u>reflects</u> off the sand.

3. <u>People</u> should go to the beach <u>early</u> in the day <u>or</u> late in the day.

4. Even at those times, <u>sunbathers</u> should be very careful about being overexposed to the <u>sun</u>.

5. Children <u>love</u> to play in the sand and <u>are</u> unaware of the intensity of the sun.

6. <u>I</u> can just hear people complaining about <u>their</u> sunburn. <u>Ouch!</u>

7. <u>It</u> is <u>wise</u> to avoid the <u>sun</u> around noon.

II. SENTENCE PARTS (30)
(Page 187 Answers)

Identify the part of speech of each underlined word.

1. I <u>am</u> a loyal baseball <u>fan</u>, <u>but</u> my team is really <u>awful</u> this year!

2. The <u>coach</u> is doing all he can do.

3. The players <u>are</u> serious fighters and <u>have</u> good <u>team</u> spirit, but nothing <u>seems</u> to help.

4. The <u>players</u> are very <u>young</u>, but I'm not sure that's a good excuse.

5. They don't have the <u>skill</u> to be champions.

6. Maybe it's their training that's at fault; I <u>really</u> don't know.

7. Too many of the players are injured, and <u>others</u> just <u>throw</u> the <u>ball</u> <u>away</u>.

8. <u>I</u> am really disappointed.

9. However, I <u>will be</u> a baseball fan <u>through good times and bad times</u>.

10. I <u>watch</u> the <u>team</u>, and I don't understand the <u>mistakes</u>.

11. They pitch <u>well</u>; they <u>hit</u> well; <u>they</u> run like lightning.

12. Their coach <u>gives</u> good <u>directions</u>.

13. Their captain pulls the team together <u>with tough pep talks</u>.

14. Next season, my team will be champions again! I <u>know</u> it!

III. SENTENCE TYPES (5)
(Page 188 Answers)

Identify the kind of sentence in the examples below.

1. Janet wants ice cream every night!

2. When she has ice cream nightly, she gains weight.

3. Do you like to have ice cream daily?

4. Do not have ice cream daily!

5. If you want to be slim like Janet, you must exercise and limit how often you have ice cream.

IV. SENTENCE PATTERNS (5)
(Page 189 Answers)

Identify the pattern of the sentences below: simple, compound, complex, compound/complex.

1. My uncle loved his wife very much and wanted a big family.

2. Although he adored children, his wife didn't want any.

3. Because my uncle had many sisters and brothers, he also had many nieces and nephews.

4. All of these children benefited from his love and generosity.

5. Because my uncle was so kind and loving, his nieces and nephews visited him often, and they showered him with love.

V. PUNCTUATION (20)
(Page 189-190 Answers)

Insert the missing punctuation marks.

1. Patricia who is my best friend lived in a small, one-room apartment in the West Village in New York City.

2. She had five cats that she took in from the street. Theyre so sweet.

3. About two times a month and on some holidays July 4th, Labor Day, her sister would drive Patricia and her cats to their childhood home in upstate New York.

4. One day, Patricia took a dog in from the street then, she took another one.

5. She didn't want two dogs and five cats in her small apartment so she decided to leave New York City for a place where her cats and dogs would have more freedom.

6. She looked for a home in several states New York, Vermont, and New Hampshire she found nothing suitable that she could afford.

7. Luckily her brother gave her some money, and she had a house built in the woods near her family's home a perfect location for her and her animals.

8. Its fabulous that you will be living near us, said her sister.

9. Patricia said I am so excited

10. How can one person be so lucky

11. Now the dogs and the cats come and go through a dog door in that beautiful, old, and well built barn.

12. Additionally, Patricia is near a library that has many books about animals including her favorite book, Animal Magnetism by Rita Mae Brown.

13. Im so happy that Patricia was able to create a home that she and her animals love.

VI. WORD CHOICES (20)
(Page 191-192 Answers)

Correct the following sentences (punctuation, correct word or tense).

1. Seeing that I was really pail, my boyfriend asked me if I felt alright.

2. I no that he cares about me, and I didn't want too worry him.

3. I taught about telling him.

4. He must not here about it from other people.

5. Dont worry; its not really bad news.

6. We all ready discussed these situations.

7. I don't have allot of time to think about the affect of the news.

8. Once the situation is clarified, than, we need to make much decisions.

9. We have to think about wear will live and who's family can help us financially.

10. I asked my college counselor for advise, and she said that it's important that our families except us with love.

11. My sister, whose all ways so difficult to please, is happy about this.

12. After all, this is a very serious situation; my parents gave me permission to marry my boyfriend!

I. WORDS (20)
(Page 181 Exercises)

1. The extremely hot sun is burning everyone who is sitting on the beach.

extremely	adverb
hot	adjective
is burning	verb
on	preposition

2. Sunscreen and umbrellas aren't effective against the skin-damaging rays because the sun reflects off the sand.

umbrellas	noun
skin-damaging	adjective
reflects	verb

3. People should go to the beach early in the day or late in the day.

people	noun
early	adverb
or	conjunction

4. Even at those times, sunbathers should be very careful about being overexposed to the sun.

sunbathers	noun
sun	noun

5. Children love to play in the sand and are unaware of the intensity of the sun.

love	verb
are	verb

6. I can just hear people complaining about their sunburn. Ouch!

I	pronoun
their	pronoun
Ouch	interjection

7. It is wise to avoid the sun around noon.

It	pronoun
wise	adjective
sun	noun

II. SENTENCE PARTS (30)
(Page 182 Exercises)

1. I <u>am</u> a loyal baseball <u>fan, but</u> my team is really <u>awful</u> this year!
   am   verb
   fan   noun, subject complement
   but   coordinating conjunction
   awful   adjective

2. The <u>coach</u> is doing all he can do.
   coach   noun subject

3. The players <u>are</u> serious fighters and <u>have</u> good <u>team</u> spirit, but nothing <u>seems</u> to help.
   are   verb
   have   verb
   team   adjective
   seems   verb

4. The <u>players</u> are very <u>young,</u> but I'm not sure that's a good excuse.
   players   noun, subject
   young   adjective, subject complement

5. They don't have the <u>skill</u> to be champions.
   skill   noun, direct object

6. Maybe it's their training that's at fault; I <u>really</u> don't know.
   really   adverb

7. Too many of the players are injured, and <u>others</u> just <u>throw</u> the <u>ball</u> <u>away</u>.
   others   noun, subject
   throw   verb
   ball   noun, direct object
   away   adverb

8. <u>I</u> am really disappointed.
   I   pronoun, subject

9. However, I <u>will be</u> a baseball fan <u>through good times and bad times</u>.
   will be   verb
   through good times and bad times   prepositional phrase

10. I <u>watch</u> the <u>team</u>, and I don't understand the <u>mistakes</u>.
watch   verb
team   noun, direct object
mistakes   noun, direct object

11. They pitch <u>well</u>; they <u>hit</u> well; <u>they</u> run like lightning.
well   adverb
hit   verb
they   pronoun, subject

12. Their coach <u>gives</u> good <u>directions</u>.
gives   verb
directions   noun, direct object

13. Their captain pulls the team together <u>with tough pep talks.</u>
with tough pep talks   prepositional phrase

14. Next season, my team will be champions again! I <u>know</u> it!
know   verb

III. SENTENCE TYPES (5)
(Page 183 Exercises)

1. Janet wants ice cream every night!
Exclamatory

2. When Janet has ice cream nightly, she gains weight.
Declarative

3. Do you like to have ice cream daily?
Interrogative

4. Do not have ice cream daily!
Imperative

5. If you want to be slim like Janet, you must exercise and limit how often you have ice cream.
Declarative

IV. SENTENCE PATTERNS (5)
(Page 183 Exercises)

1. My uncle loved his wife very much and wanted a big family.
   Simple sentence

2. Although he adored children, his wife didn't want any.
   Complex sentence

3. Because my uncle had many sisters and brothers, he also had many nieces and nephews.
   Complex sentence

4. All of these children benefited from his love and generosity.
   Simple sentence

5. Because my uncle was so kind and loving, his nieces and nephews visited him often, and they showered him with love.
   Complex/compound sentence

V. PUNCTUATION (20)
(Page 183-184 Exercises)

1. Patricia, who is my best friend, lived in a small, one-room apartment in the West Village in New York City.
   Two commas needed

2. She had five cats that she took in from the street. They're so sweet.
   Apostrophe/contraction—they're

3. About two times a month and on some holidays (July 4th, Labor Day), her sister would drive Patricia and her cats to their childhood home in upstate New York.
   Parentheses

4. One day, Patricia took a dog in from the street; then, she took another one.
   Semicolon

5. She didn't want two dogs and five cats in her small apartment, so she decided to leave New York City for a place where her cats and dogs would have more freedom.
Comma before coordinating conjunction—so

6. She looked for a home in several states: New York, Vermont, and New Hampshire. **She** found nothing suitable that she could afford.
Colon—states: New
Period and capital letter—Hampshire. She

7. Luckily, her brother gave her some money, and she had a house built in the woods near her family's **home—a** perfect location for her and her animals.
Comma—Luckily,
Dash or comma

8. **"It's** fabulous that you will be living near us," said her sister.
Apostrophe—It's
Quotation marks

9. Patricia said, **"I am so excited!"**
Comma after said or colon after said
Quotation marks
Exclamation mark

10. How can one person be so lucky**?**
Question mark

11. Now**,** the dogs and the cats come and go through a dog door in that beautiful, old, and well-built barn.
Comma after Now,
Hyphen—well-built

12. Additionally, Patricia is near a library that has many books about animals including her favorite book, *Animal Magnetism* by Rita Mae Brown.
Italics for title of book

13. I'm so happy that Patricia was able to create a home that she and her animals love.
Apostrophe—I'm

VI. WORD CHOICES (20)
(Page 185 Exercises)

1. Seeing that I was really <u>pail</u>, my boyfriend asked me if I felt <u>alright</u>.
   pale
   all right

2. I <u>no</u> that he cares about me, and I didn't want <u>too</u> worry him.
   know
   to

3. I <u>taught</u> about telling him.
   thought

4. He must not <u>here</u> about it from other people.
   hear

5. <u>Dont</u> worry; <u>its</u> not really bad news.
   Don't
   it's

6. We <u>all ready</u> discussed <u>these</u> situations.
   already
   this

7. I don't have <u>allot</u> of time to think about the <u>affect</u> of the news.
   a lot
   effect

8. Once the situation is clarified, <u>than</u>, we need to make <u>much</u> decisions.
   then
   many

9. We have to think about <u>wear</u> <u>will</u> live and <u>who's</u> family can help us financially.
   where
   we'll
   whose

10. I asked my college counselor for <u>advise</u>, and she said that it's important our families <u>except</u> us with love.
advice
accept

11. My sister, <u>whose</u> <u>all ways</u> so difficult to please, is happy about this.
who's
always

12. After all, this is a very serious situation; my parents gave me permission to marry my boyfriend!
All correct

Notes

Our language is funny–a fat chance and a slim chance are the same thing.

—J. Gustav White

Notes

Words have a longer life than deeds.

—Pindar

Chapter 15

Post-Test Exercises and Answers

Post-Test Exercises

Now is the time for a final check. Complete the post-test one section at a time. Rejoice if you score all correct. If you have fewer than all correct, review the relevant chapter again. When you feel confident, take the post-test again. There are many excellent web sites that include definitions of terms and practice tests. Additional instruction and practice will help you to become the best writer you can be. So, let's begin.

I. WORDS (20) errors
(Page 202-203 Answers)

Identify the **parts of speech** (A V CAPPIN) of the words underlined.

1. <u>Wow!</u> The <u>party</u> was <u>unbelievably</u> great!

2. I'll bet that <u>everyone</u> there, except me, had at least one <u>visible</u> tattoo.

3. Some people even <u>had</u> those <u>earrings</u> that stretch ear lobes.

4. Men had <u>long</u> hair, and <u>women</u> had short hair.

5. The food was excellent <u>and</u> all vegetarian.

6. One <u>of</u> the surprises was that there <u>were</u> no alcoholic beverages, and smoking wasn't allowed.

7. Everyone was_incredibly_ friendly and considerate.

8. The band was fabulous and played for <u>hours</u> and hours <u>without</u> a break!

9. The <u>kid</u> that <u>I</u> like was there, and we danced for hours!

10. This was a <u>very</u> <u>special</u> night for me, and I just <u>may have found</u> my partner for life!

II. SENTENCE PARTS (30)
(Page 203-204 Answers)

Identify how the underlined words are **functioning** (for example, CVS) in these sentences.

1. <u>Music</u> always <u>soothes</u> my <u>soul</u>.

2. I <u>really</u> <u>do love</u> all kinds <u>of music</u>.

3. I <u>have studied</u> <u>guitar, ukulele, banjo, and piano.</u>

4. I <u>play</u> the saxophone <u>and</u> <u>the</u> flute.

5. <u>Playing</u> with a band <u>is</u> one <u>of my dreams</u>.

6. <u>I</u> don't <u>often</u> sing <u>in front</u> <u>of other people</u>.

7. Actually I'm kind of shy, <u>but</u> when it comes to music, my personality just <u>grows</u>, and I <u>can put</u> on a good show.

8. I <u>will study</u> instrumental and <u>vocal</u> <u>music</u> in college.

9. I'<u>ve written</u> a few <u>songs</u>—melody and words—which were performed <u>by a local rock group.</u>

10. <u>Music</u> will <u>always</u> be a <u>very</u> important <u>part</u> of my life.

III. SENTENCE TYPES (5)
(Page 204-205 Answers)

Indicate whether the following sentences are declarative, imperative, interrogative, or exclamatory.

1. We heard the slow rumbling of the thunder, and we knew that the storm wasn't far away.

2. Should we try to beat the storm?

3. Mom shouted, "Before you get into your car, you must listen to the weather forecast!"

4. Suddenly, the sky lit up. Wow! That lightening is amazing!

5. Within minutes, the television announcer warned of severe rain and flooding.

IV. SENTENCE PATTERNS (5)
(Page 205 Answers)

Identify the patterns of the following sentences: simple, compound, complex, compound/complex.

1. I can't wait to swim in the ocean, but the waves are very rough today.

2. I'm a strong swimmer; however, with both a strong undercurrent and huge waves, I get really scared.

3. Because the lifeguards are alert and competent, I feel brave, and I dive into the waves.

4. It's amazing to see all of the children fearlessly playing in the water.

5. When the ocean is calm and warm, I really enjoy the waves.

V. PUNCTUATION (20)
(Page 205-206 Answers)

Insert the correct punctuation.

1. We were nine years old and I thought they were my friends but they were out to trick me.

2. They left scary notes signed "The Paw!"

3. It was so scary to receive these messages I didnt know who was sending them.

4. I couldnt imagine that my friends would scare me like this.

5. They wrote a riddle telling me to go into the garage at night they said I would find a treasure.

6. I didnt want to go into the dark garage however I surely didnt want them to think I was scared.

7. So I gathered my courage my flashlight and my baseball bat and I went into the dark garage.

8. The heavy door creaked eerily I pulled it open.

9. Although terrified of the darkness I was hopeful that Id find a treasure.

10. When I opened the mysterious looking box on the table, I was stunned!

11. In it was a smelly rotten apple pie

VI. WORD CHOICES (20)
(Page 206-207 Answers)

Some of the challenges below are discussed in this guide. Clarification of others is easy to find in dictionaries. Find and correct the errors in word choice. Not all sentences have errors.

1. The hugely popular musical husband and wife team Sonny and Cher Bono hosted a very sucesful television show in the 1970s.

2. "I Got You, Babe" is won of there biggest hits.

3. In addition to being immensely entertaining musicians, they wear a great comedy team.

4. They also delighted and enthralled the audience when sharing bits of family life including bringing they're daughter Chastity onto there show.

5. The fans grew to love the family, so when Sonny and Cher announced their divorce, the fans reacted with concern four them.

6. As many years have past, Cher moved on with her career and her personal life; Sonny died, and Chastity faced an life-altering decision.

7. Chastity announced to the public that she know longer wanted to live what she felt was an inauthentic life as a female and would began the process of physically transitioning into a men.

8. While transitioning, Chastity changed her name too Chaz.

9. Chaz have know completed the transition and is legally an man.

10. He has become an extremely affective advocate fore transgender men and woman.

11. His courage and optimism, good humor and charm are enchanting fans and creating virulent opponents. His not bothering anyone, so why can't people just leave him alone.

I. WORDS (20)
(Page 197 Exercises)

1. <u>Wow!</u> The <u>party</u> was <u>unbelievably</u> great!
   Wow—interjection
   party—noun
   unbelievably—adverb

2. I'll bet that <u>everyone</u> there, except me, had at least one <u>visible</u> tattoo.
   everyone—pronoun
   visible—adjective

3. Some people even <u>had</u> those <u>earrings</u> that stretch ear lobes.
   had—verb
   earrings—noun

4. Men had <u>long</u> hair, and <u>women</u> had short hair.
   long—adjective
   women—noun

5. The food was excellent <u>and</u> all vegetarian.
   and—conjunction

6. One <u>of</u> the surprises was that there <u>were</u> no alcoholic beverages, and smoking wasn't allowed.
   of—preposition
   were—verb

7. Everyone was <u>incredibly</u> friendly and considerate.
   incredibly—adverb

8. The band was fabulous and played for <u>hours</u> and hours <u>without</u> a break!
   hours—noun
   without—preposition

9. The <u>kid</u> that <u>I</u> like was there, and we danced for hours!
   kid—noun
   I—pronoun

10. This was a <u>very</u> <u>special</u> night for me, and I just <u>may have found</u> my partner for life!
    very—adverb
    special—adjective
    may have found—verb

II. SENTENCE PARTS (30)
(Page 198 Exercises)

1. <u>Music</u> always <u>soothes</u> my <u>soul</u>.
   Music—subject
   soothes—verb/predicate
   soul—direct object

2. I <u>really</u> <u>do love</u> all kinds <u>of music</u>.
   really—adverb
   do love—verb
   of music—adjective prepositional phrase

3. I <u>have studied</u> <u>guitar, ukulele, banjo, and piano.</u>
   have studied—verb
   guitar, ukulele, banjo, and piano—direct objects

4. I <u>play</u> the saxophone <u>and</u> <u>the</u> flute.
   play—verb
   and—conjunction
   the—adjective

5. <u>Playing</u> with a band <u>is</u> one <u>of my dreams</u>.
   Playing—subject
   is—verb
   of my dreams—adjective prepositional phrase

6. <u>I</u> don't <u>often</u> sing <u>in front</u> <u>of other people</u>.
   I—subject
   often—adverb
   in front—adverb prepositional phrase
   of other people—adjective prepositional phrase

7. Actually I'm kind of shy, <u>but</u> when it comes to music, my personality just <u>grows</u>, and I <u>can put</u> on a good show.
but—conjunction
grows—verb
can put—verb

8. I <u>will study</u> instrumental and <u>vocal</u> <u>music</u> in college.
will study—verb
vocal—adjective
music—direct object

9. I'<u>ve written</u> a few <u>songs</u>—melody and words—which were performed <u>by a local rock group.</u>
've written—verb ('ve = have)
songs—direct object
by a local rock group—adverb prepositional phrase

10. <u>Music</u> will <u>always</u> be a <u>very</u> important <u>part</u> of my life.
music—subject
always—adverb
very—adverb
part—subjective complement

III. SENTENCE TYPES (5)
(Page 199 Exercises)

1. We heard the slow rumbling of the thunder, and we knew that the storm wasn't far away.
Declarative

2. Should we try to beat the storm?
Interrogative

3. Mom shouted, "Before you get into your car, you must listen to the weather forecast!"
Imperative

4. Suddenly, the sky lit up. Wow! That lightening is amazing!
Exclamatory

5. Within minutes, the television announcer warned of severe rain and flooding.
   Declarative

IV. SENTENCE PATTERNS (5)
(Page 199 Exercises)

1. I can't wait to swim in the ocean, but the waves are very rough today.
   Compound sentence

2. I'm a strong swimmer; however, with both a strong undercurrent and huge waves, I get really scared.
   Compound sentence

3. Because the lifeguards are alert and competent, I feel brave, and I dive into the waves.
   Complex/compound sentence

4. It's amazing to see all of the children fearlessly playing in the water.
   Simple sentence

5. When the ocean is calm and warm, I really enjoy the waves.
   Complex sentence

V. PUNCTUATION (20)
(Page 200 Exercises)

1. We were nine years old, and I thought they were my friends, but they were out to trick me.
   Two commas

2. They left notes signed, "The Paw!"
   Comma

3. It was so scary to receive these messages; I didn't know who was sending them.
   Semicolon or period or comma/coordinating conjunction, and apostrophe

4. I couldn't imagine that my friends would scare me like this.
   Apostrophe

5. They wrote a riddle telling me to go into the garage at night; they said I would find a treasure.
   Semicolon or period or comma and coordinating conjunction

6. I didn't want to go into the dark garage; however, I surely didn't want them to think I was scared.
   Apostrophe, semicolon, comma, apostrophe

7. So, I gathered my courage, my flashlight, and my baseball bat, and I went into the dark garage.
   Four commas

8. The heavy door creaked eerily; I pulled it open.
   Semicolon or period or comma and coordinating conjunction

9. Although terrified of the darkness, I was hopeful that I'd find a treasure.
   Comma, apostrophe

10. When I opened the mysterious-looking box on the table, I was stunned!
    Hyphen

11. In it was a smelly, rotten apple pie!
    Comma, exclamation mark

VI. WORD CHOICES (20)
(Page 201 Exercises)

1. The hugely popular musical husband and wife team Sonny and Cher Bono hosted a very **successful** television show in the 1970s.

2. "I Got You Babe" is **one** of **their** biggest hits.

3. In addition to being immensely entertaining musicians, they **were** a great comedy team.

4. They also delighted and enthralled the audience when sharing bits of family life including bringing **their** daughter Chastity onto **their** show.

5. The fans grew to love the family, so when Sonny and Cher announced their divorce, the fans reacted with concern **for** them.

6. As many years have **passed**, Cher moved on with her career and her personal life; Sonny died, and Chastity faced **a** life-altering decision.

7. Chastity announced to the public that she **no** longer wanted to live what she felt was an inauthentic life as a female and would **begin** the process of physically transitioning into a **man**.

8. While transitioning, Chastity changed her name **to** Chaz.

9. Chaz **has** **now** completed the transition and is legally **a** man.

10. He has become an extremely **effective** advocate **for** transgender men and **women**.

11. His courage and optimism, good humor and charm are enchanting fans as well as, sadly, creating virulent opponents. **He's** not bothering anyone, so why can't people just leave him alone.

Notes

Grasp the subject; the words will follow.

—Cato the Elder

Chapter 16

Answers to Chapter Exercises

The answers to the exercises are placed alphabetically according to the letter and number identifying them.

A1 Adjectives (35 adjectives)
(Page 16–17 Exercises)

1. I am a <u>loyal</u> baseball fan, but <u>my</u> team is really <u>awful</u> <u>this</u> year!

2. The <u>dedicated</u> coach is doing all he can do.

3. <u>The</u> players are <u>serious</u> fighters and have <u>good</u> <u>team</u> spirit, but nothing seems to help.

4. <u>The</u> players are very <u>young</u>, but I'm not sure that's <u>a good</u> excuse.

5. They don't seem to have <u>the</u> skill needed to be <u>national</u> champions.

6. Maybe it's <u>their</u> training that's at fault; I really don't know.

7. Too many <u>good</u> players are <u>injured,</u> and others seem to just throw the ball away.

8. What I do know is that I am really <u>hurt</u> and <u>disappointed</u> by <u>careless</u> players and <u>rude</u> fans.

9. However, I will always be <u>an avid</u> baseball fan through <u>good</u> times and <u>bad</u> times.

10. I look forward to <u>next</u> season when I know (like <u>a true baseball</u> fan) that <u>my</u> team will be champions once again!

C1 Comma
(Page 108 Exercises)

Competitive Sports by Fred Worell

1. I like watching sports.

2. Mostly, I like watching basketball and football.

3. My favorite basketball team is Oklahoma City Thunder.

4. My favorite football team is the New York Giants.

5. I also like playing sports with my friends.

6. My favorite sports to play are basketball, football, and handball.

7. I like watching sports because they are competitive.

8. I like playing because I like competing against my friends, and it also keeps me in shape.

9. Also, it's a lot of fun to beat my friends.

10. Playing sports teaches me how to work with others.

C2 Comma Placement
(Page 108–109 Exercises)

Leaving Taiwan for the USA by Peter (Chein-chang) Li

1. I left my parents and Taiwan and moved to the United States twenty-eight years ago.

2. I brought my new wife to the United States, and without any relatives or friends around us, we started a new adventure.

3. I departed my job as a cargo ship sailor, and she left her nursing job.

4. By learning about the American experience from television, I had promised her that the USA was full of opportunities to learn English, look for jobs, and live in a big house.

5. We hoped that we would survive and save money in the bank. Then, we would be able to buy a used car and drive it to supermarkets, the laundry, and to furniture stores.

6. Eventually, we will buy our house in the suburbs and move to our sweet home with our car.

7. We will have children, and they will play baseball on our green grass in our backyard.

8. We want to make our dreams come true in this journey in spite of the opposite opinions from families.

9. Now, many years have passed by, and we have fulfilled our goals.

10. We have experienced that life in America is like a variety of flavors; sometimes, it is sour like hot-and-sour soup, sweet like ice cream, bitter like bitter herbs, and hot like Mexican hot chili.

11. We understand the laws and respond to Court Summons to pay parking tickets.

12. I often parked the car where it was convenient for me; consequently, I learned the lesson to obey parking signs by sitting in the courts and paying the fines.

13. We are grateful to the volunteers for teaching us English because we were so eager to adapt to this new life.

14. Our English teachers were from the local senior citizen organizations, and the classrooms were the local libraries and supermarkets. That was our first schooling experience in the USA.

CO Contractions
(Page 98 Exercises)

Krystal by Elias Salaam

1. Krystal's = Krystal is

2. I've = I have

3. She's = she is

4. I'm = I am

5. I've = I have

6. I'd = I could/would
   won't = will not
   it's = it is

7. none

8. She's = she is
   don't = do not

9. none

10. We're = We are

11. none

12. She's = She is

Chapter 16: *Answers to Chapter Exercises*

CW1 Word Choices
(Page 144–145 Exercises)

1. its (possessive)

2. their (possessive)

3. a lot (many), too

4. all ready (ready works on its own)

5. affect (verb)

6. then (time)

7. whose (possessive)

8. accept

9. advice, it's

10. then (time) than (contrast)

Now, read about Lori tending her garden.

11. I am **an** early riser.

12. One of the first things I **do** when I wake up in the morning is water my garden.

13. I begin with the window boxes on the west side of the house and **then** work my way over to the mixed perennial beds in the front of the house.

14. Once a week, if it is **really** hot, I'll water the hedges surrounding the beds.

15. This entire process can take over **an** hour, but I don't **mind**.

16. I prefer using **a** hand-held wand **to** just turning on **a** sprinkler.

17. I enjoy being in the garden early in the **morning** when **it's quiet** and still.

18. Tending my garden gives me time to think before I start my day. **No errors**

CW2 Word Choices
(Page 148-149 Exercises)

1. My son likes California, ~~in~~ which he says is a dreamland.

2. Martin Luther King, Jr. wants his children to enjoy a life ~~in~~ that he longed for himself.

3. President Obama gives a speech, ~~one in~~ which motivates an entire nation to act.

4. Sam was *going* to India to study yoga.

5. In *The New York Times* article "NYC Firemen are Heroes," *a journalist* reports on three huge fires in one night.

CW3 Word Choices
(Page 149 Exercises)

Basketball Is My Game by Mario Leopold

1. My favorite basketball <u>team</u> is the New York Knicks.

2. I played basketball at age eleven.

3. I played in the Nike Swish Tournament in 2006; we <u>lost</u> in the playoffs.

4. My love <u>for</u> the game <u>grew</u> as a I got older.

5. I have seven basketball <u>trophies</u>.

6. My favorite movie <u>is</u> "He Got Game," a <u>film</u> about basketball.

7. I <u>went</u> as far as Montreal <u>for</u> a basketball game.

8. Montreal has <u>a</u> <u>lot</u> of ball players from different cultures.

9. My favorite basketball player is Derrick Rose.

10. Derrick Rose plays for the Chicago Bulls NBA team.

D1 Diagramming
(Page 128 Exercises)

1. Birds | fly

2. Birds | fly _swiftly_

3. birds | fly — _Blue_ ... _swiftly_

4. birds | fly — _Chubby_ _blue_ ... _gracefully_

5. birds | fly — _Chubby_ _blue_ ... _through_ trees _the_ ... _gracefully_

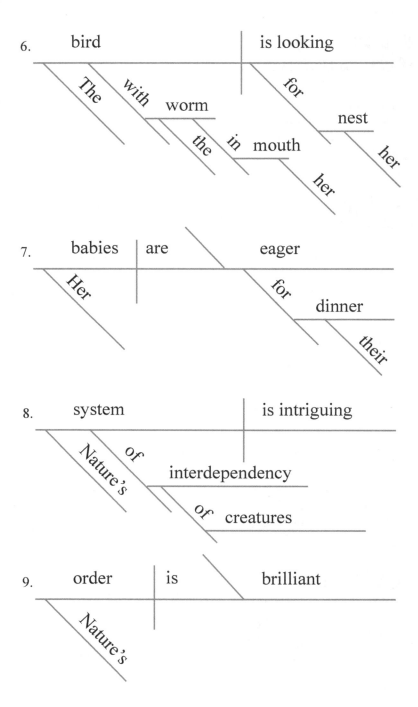

6. The bird is looking with worm the in mouth her for nest her

7. Her babies are eager for dinner their

8. Nature's system of interdependency of creatures is intriguing

9. Nature's order is brilliant

10.

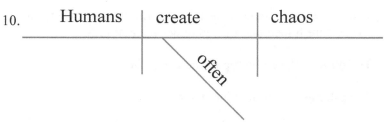

| Humans | create | chaos |

often

K1 Kinds of Sentences
(Page 74 Exercises)

1. Declarative

2. Imperative

3. Exclamatory

4. Interrogative

5. Interrogative

6. Interrogative

7. Declarative

8. Imperative

9. Imperative

10. Exclamatory

LD1 Logical Development
(Page 10 Exercises)

1. I have to make my bed.

2. I need to get clean sheets and pillowcases from the closet.

3. Ready to place the linens on the bed, I move the bed away from the wall; this allows me to reach around it more easily.

4. The bottom sheet needs to be stretched; now, it fits tightly around the corners.

5. The top sheet is placed neatly over the bottom sheet, and the corners are folded and tucked under the mattress.

6. The quilt is placed on top of the clean sheets.

7. The pillows are slipped into the cases.

8. The pillows are placed on top of the cover.

9. Next, I'll push the bed back against the wall.

10. The bed looks very neat now that I'm finished.

M1 Modifiers
(Page 54 Exercises)

1. the = adjective—which geraniums? (modifies noun)
   pink = adjective—which geraniums? (modifies noun)
   very = adverb—how beautiful? (modifies adjective)
   beautiful = adjective—which petunias? (modifies noun)
   purple = adjective—which petunias? (modifies noun)

2. serious = adjective—what kind of gardening? (modifies noun)
   incredibly = adverb—how strenuous? (modifies adjective)
   strenuous = adjective—what kind of work? (modifies noun)
   immensely = adverb—how rewarding? (modifies adjective)

3. early = adverb—when in the morning? (modifies prepositional phrase acting as an adverb)
   in the morning = adverb prepositional phrase—when going? (modifies going)
   delicate = adjective—what kind of flowers? (modifies noun

4. optimists = adjective, subject complement—what kind of gardeners— (modifies noun gardeners)
   by planting = adverb prepositional phrase—demonstrate how? (modifies verb demonstrate)

M&V1 Mood and Voice
(Page 69 Exercises)

1. I would help my brother meet hip kids if I <u>were</u> at his college.

2. If only the kids in high school <u>were</u> to give him a chance, they would know what a sweetheart he really is.

3. If he <u>were</u> straight, bullies would leave him alone.

4. A call was received by the Dean of Students about the bullying. (passive voice)

5. My mom called the police. (active voice)

6. The police notified the school. (active voice)

7. Those ugly, mean weaklings victimized my brother. (active voice)

8. My heart was aching for my little brother. (passive voice)

9. Joining the LGBTQI club helped him feel less frightened and lonely.

10. The LGBTQI adviser and club members offered support, friendship, and protection. (active voice)

P1 Punctuation Apostrophe
(Page 101 Exercises)

1. It's—contraction for it is—omit the letter I, and add an apostrophe as a placeholder for omitted letter

2. Speaker's—singular possessive—one speaker

3. Teachers'—plural possessive—many teachers' lessons

4. Students'—plural possessive—many students agrees with they're

5. No apostrophes

6. Days'—plural possessive—many indicates plural

7. Students'—plural possessive

8. Professors'—plural possessive

9. Would've—contraction for would have—omit the letters HA, and add an apostrophe as a placeholder for omitted letters

10. Shouldn't—contraction for should not—omit the letter O, and add an apostrophe as a placeholder for omitted letter
He's—contraction for he is—omit the letter I, and add an apostrophe as a placeholder for omitted letter
She's—contraction for she is—omit the letter I, and add an apostrophe as a placeholder for omitted letter

P2 Punctuation
(Page 117–118 Exercises)

1. C

2. C

3. The new farmers were very pleased to find a well-built barn on the property that they had just purchased.

4. The massive, antique clock stood proudly in the hallway.

5. The principal said, "Please, raise your hand."

6. C

7. C

8. As soon as the sun rises, the fog will begin to disappear.

9. C

10. C

P3 Punctuation
(Page 118–119 Exercises)

Soccer, Once My Favorite Sport by Jovian Rutherford

1. My favorite sport of all time is soccer.

2. When I was a chil<u>d,</u> I wanted to be a soccer player.

3. Now that I am grow<u>n,</u> I don<u>'t</u> want to be a soccer player anymore.

4. People used to sa<u>y,</u> "You should be a basketball player. You're too tall to play soccer."

5. I never listened much to what people had to say because soccer was my passion.

6. When I was younge<u>r,</u> I used to play soccer in the park all the time.

7. My dad used to bring me to Marine Park in Brookly<u>n,</u> N.Y. every day after school to practice soccer.

8. Even though I don<u>'t</u> watch soccer anymore on televisio<u>n,</u> I like to keep up with wha<u>t's</u> going on in the leagues today.

9. I am from a Caribbean background where soccer is the most popular sport.

10. In the Caribbea<u>n,</u> we refer to soccer as football because we use our feet to play.

11. Although all my relatives were once soccer player<u>s,</u> no one made it professionally.

12. After moving to the United State<u>s,</u> I found inspiration in watching basketball.

13. The similarities between soccer and basketball are aggressive players and constant running.

14. The difference between basketball and soccer is in basketball you use your hand<u>s,</u> and in soccer it is strictly about using your feet.

15. On a soccer field, there are eleven players on the field for each team including a goalkeeper also referred to as a goalie.

16. In basketball<u>,</u> only five players are allowed on the basketball court for each team.

17. In soccer, scoring a goal is one point; in basketball, scoring a basket is two or three points.

18. I think I will change my favorite sport from soccer to basketball because soccer is less popular in America.

19. What is your favorite sport<u>?</u>

20. Is soccer your favorite sport, too?

PC1 Pronoun Cases (Page 67 Exercises)

1. I

2. She and I

3. she

4. ourselves

5. her

6. her

7. her, him, and me

8. his

9. He

10. His
    them

11. his

PC2 Pronoun Cases
(Page 68 Exercises)

1. My friend Fran and **I** are always dieting.

2. **She and I** like to go out for ice cream every evening.

3. I love socializing with **her**, but when we're together, the temptation to eat ice cream becomes overwhelming, and **we** often give in.

4. We've worked so hard to lose weight, so **she and I** feel really disappointed in **ourselves** when we see the pounds coming back.

5. My doctor weighs **me** every time I go to see **him.**

6. Fran's doctor weighs **her** too.

7. Because **she and I** eat a variety of healthy foods, that's not the problem.

8. It's about quantity; **she and I** just eat too much.

9. If you have advice for **us,** please, call **her and me**, and share **your** ideas.

10. **She and I** really try to behave **ourselves**, and **we're** going to succeed this time!

PP Prepositional Phrases
(Page 54-55 Exercises)

Violence with Guns by Godfrey Sakyi

1. Gun control is one (of the most controversial issues) (in our society).

2. Gun violence (in the country) has dramatically increased.

3. Is the Second Amendment (of the Bill of Rights) also a factor (in gun violence)?

4. Drive-by shootings and gang shootings are committed almost every day.

5. Gangs (in the United States) are more violent and deadly, hence, increasing gun violence (in our society).

6. Can the government stop or reduce the rapid growth (of gun violence) (in the country)?

7. The rise (of gun violence) shouldn't be blamed (on violent games, movies, television programs, and song lyrics). The family backgrounds (of the violators) should be considered.

8. Most crimes (in the United States) are committed (with a gun).

9. What do you think are the causes (of gun violence) (in our society)?

10. What can we do to reduce gun violence (in our country)?

SENTENCE PARTS
S1a Subject Verb Agreement
(Page 63-64 Exercises)

1. run (to agree with plural subject players)

2. exercises (to agree with singular subject player)

3. hire (to agree with plural teams)

4. helps (to agree with singular yoga)

5. assists (to agree with singular yoga)

6. spots (to agree with singular teacher)

7. places (to agree with teacher)
   needs (to agree with singular "that," which refers to body)

8. is needed (to agree with singular attention)
   approaches (to agree with player)

9. hire (to agree with plural teachers)
   is (to agree with singular no one)

10. hear (to agree with plural fans)
    do (to agree with plural players)
    want (to agree with plural fans)

S1b Subject/Verb Agreement
(Page 64-65 Exercises)

The Enjoyment of Music by José de la Rosa

1. I always <u>enjoy</u> going to a good music concert, collecting records, and creating music.

2. I <u>love</u> different styles of music from punk rock, metal, electronic, old school hip hop to more traditional styles like blues, classical, and native music.

3. I could go to an electronic music party and <u>dance</u> all night or <u>see</u> a punk band and pogo through the whole show.

4. I usually go out with my girl; she is the greatest companion. We always <u>have</u> a good time.

5. She is more into electronic (techno) music than I am. (correct)

6. We <u>are</u> thinking about going to two big festivals this year: Coachella in California and Maryland Death Fest in Baltimore.

7. We just bought tickets to see Killing Joke on April 19th at Irving Plaza. (correct)

8. Killing Joke <u>is</u> a very prolific English post-punk band that started in the early eighties.

9. I used to be a drummer and sang in a few bands; I was in a total of six bands in a period of seven years. (correct)

10. Nowadays, I'm calmer and just <u>have</u> one music project with a friend; we <u>haven't</u> played any shows yet; we <u>are</u> just in the process of creating tunes.

S1c Pronoun and Antecedent Agreement (Page 65 Exercises)

1. their

2. their

3. their

4. his

5. his
   he

S1d Subjects and Verbs (Page 66 Exercises)

1. S—Joe Namath
   V—was

2. S—position
   V—was

3. S—fans
   V—were

4. S—He
   V—was

5. S—I
   V—wanted

6. S—tickets
   V—were

7. S—price
   V—excluded

8. S—watching
   V—beats

9. S—brother
    V—loves

10. S—Dad
    V—recalls

11. S—players
    V—covered

12. S—Watching
    V—is

SE1 Sentence Errors
(Page 92 Exercises)

1. RO, Run-on (or fused)

2. F, Fragment

3. CS, Comma splice

4. RO, Run-on

5. F, Fragment

SE2 Sentence Errors
(Page 93 Exercises)

The errors in the sentences have been identified and corrected.
There are other ways of correcting them. Check the text to see if the
corrections you have made are also acceptable.

The Story in Progress by Daniel Huerta

1. Comma splice—I was going to join the Army, but my ankle operation
    delayed my plans.

2. Fragment—Because I have had an ankle problem since
    childhood, my plans for my future had to be delayed.

3. Fragment—In order to join the Army, I would have to lose a
    massive amount of weight.

4. Comma splice—I would like to be the leader of my squad in the Army. I have good leadership skills.

5. Correct—Wanting to be in the battlefield is my greatest goal.

6. Run on—Serving this country can make many proud of me. My parents and friends will be especially happy for me.

7. Fragment—Once I got the hang of things in the Army, I was thinking of joining the Marines.

8. Run on—Being in the Army is a life-changing experience. It will make me a more independent man.

9. Run on—For me, being in the military is going to be of great importance. I will become more disciplined.

10. Fragment—Serving in the military will be an adventure to be told to my family for generations.

SP1 Sentence Patterns (Page 89 Exercises)

1. Simple

2. Compound

3. Compound

4. Simple

5. Complex

6. Complex

7. Compound

8. Compound/complex

There may be variations in responses to the following; however, the correct conjunction should be used.

9. Tedra was a leader, and Elyse was a follower.

10. Tedra was a leader; consequently, Elyse was a follower.

11. Because Tedra was a leader, Elyse followed her.

SP2 Sentence Patterns
(Page 90-91 Exercises)

My After-school Life by Ayodele Finch

1. Simple

2. Simple

3. Simple

4. Compound (three independent clauses)

5. Complex

6. Simple

7. Complex

8. Complex

9. Complex/compound

10. Complex

11. Compound

12. Compound/complex

13. Complex

14. Simple

SP3 Sentence Patterns
(Page 91-92 Exercises)

Drawing by Elsa Hadad

1. Complex

2. Complex

3. Complex

4. Simple

5. Compound

6. Simple

7. Complex

8. Compound/complex

9. Simple

10. Compound/complex

11. Complex

12. Complex

V1 Verb Tenses
(Page 25 Exercises)

Tenses of regular verb **to kiss**

Past	kissed
Past perfect	had kissed
Past progressive	was/were kissing
Past perfect progressive	had been kissing
Present	kiss/kisses
Present perfect	have/has kissed
Present progressive	is/am/are kissing
Present perfect progressive	have/has been kissing

Future	will kiss
Future perfect	will have kissed
Future progressive	will be kissing
Future perfect progressive	will have been kissing

V2 Verb Tenses (Page 26 Exercises)

Irregular verb **to do**

Past	did
Past perfect	had done
Past progressive	was/were doing
Past perfect progressive	had been doing

Present	do/does
Present perfect	have/has done
Present progressive	is/am/are doing
Present perfect progressive	have/has been doing

Future	will do
Future perfect	will have done
Future progressive	will be doing
Future perfect progressive	will have been doing

V3 Verb Tenses (Page 27 Exercises)

Tenses of the verb to look

I look	we look
You look	you look
He, she, it looks	they look

V4 Consistency in Verb Tense (16 changes) (Page 28 Exercises)

1. There once <u>was</u> a dog <u>named</u> Tucker.

2. He <u>was</u> found as a puppy in the East Village of New York City several years ago.

3. Nobody <u>wanted</u> him except one person who <u>took</u> him home even though she had two other dogs at that time.

4. Within several years, he <u>grew</u> up to be a beautiful black dog with silky fur.

5. When he <u>was</u> a puppy, he <u>loved</u> the water and could swim long distances.

6. When he was a frisky puppy, he often <u>jumped</u> into a canoe or <u>swam</u> along side it.

7. He also <u>loved</u> to fetch sticks and go after tennis balls thrown into the water.

8. When he was a little dog, he <u>disappeared</u> into the woods around the water and would be gone for close to an hour.

9. Our guess was that he <u>was</u> probably chasing an animal.

10. Tucker <u>was</u> fearless in nature but <u>was</u> afraid of brooms and people's feet.

11. He <u>lived</u> a long life.

V5 Consistency in Verb Tense (Page 29 Exercises)

The following corrections are not the only possibilities. Check the chapter to see what other corrections would be acceptable.

Hurricane Sandy by Amer Yahia

1. On October 22, 2012, the hurricane known as Sandy flooded New York City, New Jersey, and other parts of Pennsylvania.

2. Properties were damaged due to Sandy.

3. Many people lost their homes.

4. The people were placed in temporary shelters.

5. The government had to pay fifty-four billion dollars to aid the Sandy storm victims.

6. There were at least 149 people confirmed dead including all states.

7. The subways had been flooded and were closed.

8. Airlines services had been cancelled.

9. Mayor Bloomberg had closed most of the gas stations in New York City and New Jersey.

10. After all that, President Barack Obama gathered with New Jersey Governor Chris Christie to go over the aftermath of the hurricane.

W1 Parts of Speech
(Page 39 Exercises)

1. adjective (modifies flowers—answers what kind of?)

2. verb (tells past tense)

3. noun (names something)

4. verb (tells present tense)

5. adjective (modifies stems)

6. noun (names something)

7. verb (tells present tense)

8. noun (object of preposition)

9. adjective (modifies containers—answers what kind of?)

10. verb (tells future tense)

Photo © Filaphoto, 2011. Used under license from Shutterstock, Inc.

Bridges to Information

Chapter 17

Web Sites to Complement
The GPS for Writing

Practice is essential for learning. *The GPS for Writing* includes some exercises; however, you may want more practice; that's easy. There are many fun and instructive web sites. At the end of each chapter is a list of helpful web sites. The list below includes those sites and more. In fact, the list includes sites that help the entire *GPS*.

New grammar, punctuation, and structure web sites are always added to the web. Check to see which sites you find easy to understand, are fun, and are informative. Try the sites that offer instruction, practice, explanations, and quizzes with answers. Use the sites to complement the instruction in *The GPS for Writing*.

Some sites, listed below, are included in more than one subject area because they cover several topics in *The GPS for Writing: Grammar, Punctuation, and Structure*. Additionally, some of these sites will lead you to other useful sites. Some sites may have been deleted since I posted them. Have fun exploring the vast number of reliable, fun, and informative sites on the web.

Here are just a few of my favorites, listed in alphabetical order according to *GPS* subject area.

The Composing Process

http://owl.english.purdue.edu/owl/resource/587/1/
http://webtech.kennesaw.edu/jcheek4/writing.htm
http://writesite.cuny.edu/
http://voices.yahoo.com/how-write-composition-2245472.html

233

Diagramming

http://www.wisc-online.com/Objects/ViewObject.aspx?ID=WCN8207

http://grammar.ccc.commnet.edu/grammar/diagrams2/diagrams_frames.htm
Moutoux, Eugene, R. "500 Sentence Diagrams"

http://grammar.ccc.commnet.edu/grammar/diagrams/diagrams.htm

http://grammar.ccc.commnet.edu/grammar/diagrams2/diagrams_frames.htm

http://grammar.ccc.commnet.edu/grammar/diagrams2/one_pager1.htm

GPS—All Aspects of Grammar, Punctuation, and Sentence Structure

Agenda Web GPS with Exercises
http://www.agendaweb.org/

CUNY (City University of New York) Write Site
http://writesite.cuny.edu

English Grammar Lessons
http://www.english-grammar-lessons.com/

English as a Second Language
http://www.eslgold.com

Diagramming GPS all parts of the sentence with exercises
http://grammar.ccc.commnet.edu/grammar/diagrams2/diagrams_frames.htm

Grammar Girl's Quick and Dirty Tips
http://grammar.quickanddirtytips.com

Guide to Grammar & Writing
http://grammar.ccc.commnet.edu/grammar/

Basic grammar
http://grammar.about.com/od/basicsentencegrammar/Understanding_
Parts_of_Speech_and_Building_Effective_Sentences.htm

Language Arts: Go Grammar
http://classroom.jc-schools.net/basic/la-grammar.html

Moutoux, Eugene, R. "500 Sentence Diagrams"
http://www.german-latin-english.com/diagrams.htm

Purdue University Online Writing Lab
http://owl.english.purdue.edu/owl/resource

Schoolhouse Rock Grammar Videos
http://www.schoolhouserock.tv

Proofreading

http://www.lrcom.com/tips/proofreading_editing.htm

http://www.dailywritingtips.com/8-proofreading-tips-and-techniques/

http://owl.english.purdue.edu/owl/resource/561/01/

Punctuation

http://www.superteacherworksheets.com/punctuation.html

http://www.savethecomma.com/game/

http://www.oswego.org/ocsd-web/quiz/mquiz.asp?filename=kderittepun

http://grammar.quickanddirtytips.com/punctuating-questions.aspx

Sentence Parts

http://depts.dyc.edu/learningcenter/owl/sentences_core_parts.htm

Subject-verb agreement
http://grammar.quickanddirtytips.com/subject-verb-agreement.aspx

Modifiers at the beginning of a sentence
http://grammar.quickanddirtytips.com/as-like-at-beginning.aspx

Sentence Patterns

Verb Phrases
http://en.wikipedia.org/wiki/Verb_phrase
Covers all sentence patterns
http://www.eslbee.com.sentences.htm

Subordinate adverb clauses
http://www.rockpicklepublishing.com/essays/
complexsentencessubordinateclausesadverbclauses.html

http://www.eslbee.com/sentences.htm

http://grammar.quickanddirtytips.com/complex-sentences.aspx

http://grammar.quickanddirtytips.com/run-on-sentences.aspx

http://grammar.quickanddirtytips.com/sentence-fragments-grammar.aspx

http://grammar.quickanddirtytips.com/comma-splice.aspx

Sentence Types

http://www.worksheetworks.com/english/partsofspeech/sentences/
identify-types.html

http://edhelper.com/language/sentences.htm

Word Choices

http://www.drgrammar.org/frequently-asked-questions

1600 words to increase vocabulary
http://virtualsalt.com/vocablst.htm

http://www.testprepreview.com/prefixes_suffixes.htm

http://www.uefap.com/vocab/build/building.htm

http://jerz.setonhill.edu/writing/grammar-and-syntax/gender-neutral-language/

Words

Adjectives and Adverbs
http://www.youtube.com/watch?v=mYzGLzFuwxI

Conjunctions
http://www.youtube.com/watch?v=mkO87mkgcNo

Grammar Worksheets
http://www.superteacherworksheets.com

Nouns
http://www.youtube.com/watch?v=Tc-ukN1Rvb8

Nouns
http://www.youtube.com/watch?v=MZcka8Zg-uc

Verbs
http://www.youtube.com/watch?v=h4QEzJe6_ok

Verbs
http://www.youtube.com/watch?v=f2NOav4Xx1c

Notes

One of the Internet's strengths is its ability to help consumers find the right needle in a digital haystack of data.

—Jared Sandberg

_____

_____

_____

_____

_____

_____

_____

_____

_____

_____

_____

_____

_____

_____

_____

_____

_____

Index

singular indefinite personal pronouns, 35–36
slash, 116–117
spelling
    proofreading for, 9
    rules, 134–135
statement of fact, 73
statement of opinion, 73
style guides, 8, 97
subject complement (subject completer)
    defined, 48, 178
    as sentence parts, 49–50
subjects
    defined, 178
    diagramming sentences, 123–124
    exercises, 66
    nominative case pronoun, 47, 50
    as sentence part, 47
    sentence patterns and, 78–79
    subject/verb agreement, 56–57
    subject/verb agreement, exercises, 63–64
subjunctive mood, 62
subordinating conjunctions, 31
suffix, 150
superlative degree, 60
syllables, 134–135
syntax, 55

T

tense
    consistency in, 62, 164
    perfect progressive tenses, 24, 25
    perfect tenses, 22–23, 25
    simple tenses, 20–21
    word choice and placement, 147–148
"that"/"which"/"who," 141
"then"/"than," 142
"there"/"they're"/"their," 142

thesis statement, 170, 178
third person conjugation, 26–27
"thought"/"taught," 142–143
titles, capitalization for, 102–103
topic sentence, 170, 178
transitional words, 79, 164, 171–172
transitive verbs, 29–30, 45–46

U

underlining, 117
unity, 158, 164, 166

V

verbals, 38, 178
verbs
    adverbs and, 31–33
    conjugating, 26–27
    consistency in tense and number of, 62
    defined, 18–19, 178
    diagramming sentences, 123
    emphatic forms of, 25
    exercises, 25–28, 63–64, 66
    helping verbs, 45
    irregular, 25
    linking verbs, 46–47
    perfect progressive tenses, 24, 25
    perfect tenses, 22–23, 25
    progressive tenses, 23–24, 25
    regular, 24
    as sentence parts, 43, 44–47
    simple tenses, 20–21
    subject/verb agreement, 56–57, 63–64
    transitive and intransitive, 29–30, 45–46
    verb phrase, 45
    word choice and placement, 147–148
vocabulary, building, 150. *see also* word choice
voice, active/passive, 62–63, 69

W

Endorsements

Professor Feder is one of the most experienced writing teachers in all of the City University of New York, a fact obvious in the well-considered approach taken in this student-centered guide. This new edition improves on what was already a useful tool for the writing classroom by expanding into areas such as proofreading, helping students develop skills that will last a lifetime. It is accessible to students at all writing levels and useful even to the expert.

Aaron Barlow, Associate Professor of English, New York City College of Technology (CUNY), and Faculty Editor of the AAUP magazine Academe.

The GPS helps students at a variety of levels navigate the complex landscape of grammar with a user-friendly, accessible format.

Caroline Chamberlin Hellman, Associate Professor of English, New York City College of Technology (CUNY), co-author of CATskills: Mastering the CUNY CATW and College Writing

----

The GPS for Writing is very direct, easy for students to understand. will be of such help to both students and teachers.

Eleanor Y. Brown, Adjunct, Humanities Department, New Jersey Institute of Technology (NJIT)

The GPS is both instructive and user-friendly. My students, from classes in Adult Basic English through Composition with Literature, have used the GPS to instruct themselves and each other in the basics of grammar and proper language use for all levels of college communication.

Mária I. Cipriani, Adjunct Lecturer, New York City College of Technology, CUNY

The GPS by Prof. Feder helps me to understand how to write an essay. It helps me to write sentences, to know when to use the right punctuation, how to identify comma splices and run-on sentences This book guides me to write correctly.

What I like most about this book is that once you read the first few pages, you are going to want to read more. This book is easy to understand, and the content is easy to remember. My thanks to Prof. Feder for writing and sharing this book

Elsa Hadad, Student, New York City College of Technology, CUNY